SOME PEOPLE WANT TO SHOOT ME

First published 2024 by
FREMANTLE PRESS

Fremantle Press Inc. trading as Fremantle Press
PO Box 158, North Fremantle, Western Australia, 6159
fremantlepress.com.au

Copyright © Wayne Bergmann and Madelaine Dickie, 2024.

The moral rights of the authors have been asserted.

This book is copyright. Apart from any fair dealing for the purpose of private study, research, criticism or review, as permitted under the *Copyright Act*, no part may be reproduced by any process without written permission. Every reasonable effort has been made to seek permission for quotations contained herein. Please address any enquiries to the publisher.

Cover photograph by Michael Jalaru Torres.
Designed by Carolyn Brown, tendeersigh.com.au
Map by Chris Crook, Country Cartographics, ccarto.com.au

 A catalogue record for this book is available from the National Library of Australia

ISBN 9781760992378 (paperback)
ISBN 9781760992385 (ebook)

Fremantle Press is supported by the Western Australian State Government through the Department of Cultural Industries, Tourism and Sport.

Fremantle Press respectfully acknowledges the Whadjuk people of the Noongar nation as the Traditional Owners and Custodians of the land where we work in Walyalup.

SOME PEOPLE WANT TO SHOOT ME

Wayne Bergmann &
Madelaine Dickie

Warning: This book contains names of people who have passed away.

Some People Want to Shoot Me is dedicated to my wife Chris, and my children Sara, Jarred and Tessa. They have lived with the burden of my commitment to make a difference to the lives of Aboriginal people. They have endured this journey with great grace, and I am so proud of the young adults they have become. It's also dedicated to my mum, dad, brothers, sisters, aunties, uncles, nannas and in-laws, who all came into the firing line because of the path I chose. I thank them for their unwavering support and love. I'd also like to thank the people and friends who I've worked with over my years in the Kimberley—they have inspired me not to accept the lowest common denominator. They include Joe Brown, Ivan McPhee, Johnny Watson, Frank Davey, Murren Hunter, Patrick and Paul Sampi, Hitler Pamba, Stumpy Brown, Irene Davey and Annie Milgin.

—Wayne Bergmann

Contents

Introduction: Madelaine Dickie	7
Abbreviations	9
Map: The Kimberley	10
Prologue: Bilby killer	11
1: With rosaries in one hand, revolvers in the other	14
2: The shadows that don't exist	35
3: If you can make it in Fitzroy, you can make it anywhere	54
4: The frontline and the battleline	78
5: Every strong life calls forth enemies	94
6: I challenge anyone to take that kind of fire	123
7: Work hard, have fun, get shit done	156
8: Judge, jury and executioner	174
9: 'You're blackfellas, you can't run a property.'	188
10: A mind endlessly restless	194
Notes	206
Works cited	210
Select bibliography	219
Acknowledgements	222

Introduction: Madelaine Dickie

In 2014 Wayne interviewed me for a job as media and communications officer at KRED Enterprises in Broome, Western Australia. He was the chief executive. During the interview, he looked me straight in the eye and said, 'Some people want to shoot me.'

I had no idea what he was talking about.

I had no idea Broome was a battlefield, full of those wounded during the James Price Point negotiations, which, had it not been for the lead proponent's withdrawal, would have led to the construction of a giant gas plant just north of the town. Wayne had spearheaded the negotiations on behalf of Traditional Owners for that country, back when he was CEO of the Kimberley Land Council.

I knew none of this when I accepted the job. What I did learn, very quickly, was that I loved working with Wayne. He was demanding, smart, intensely political and visionary. He had assembled a team at KRED who were loyal and who shared his vision.

Over the next five years, I celebrated with Nyikina Mangala people as they were granted native title at Lanji Lanji, a place on the Martuwarra (Fitzroy River) of whistling ducks, barramundi and saltwater crocodiles. Wayne's people had been fighting to have their native title recognised for eighteen years. I accompanied ABC's Landline program to Nyikina-owned Mount Anderson

Station, to document the birth of the Kimberley Agriculture and Pastoral Company, an Aboriginal-owned pastoral venture which would come to control over seven hundred thousand hectares of the Kimberley. While not quite in the league of billionaires Gina Rinehart and Andrew 'Twiggy' Forrest, it was on its way! I became inculcated in the world of native title; addicted to the Kimberley's rich and dark history, and to its politics.

When Wayne asked me to write this story—a story of independent Aboriginal economic development—I felt his sense of urgency. It has been a privilege to work on.

Unless otherwise noted, all quotes attributed to Wayne, or others, come from interviews I conducted between 2020 and 2022. Wayne and I worked closely together on the final text. I am proud to be a co-author of his story.

Abbreviations

AML	Aboriginal Maritime Limited
ATSIC	Aboriginal and Torres Strait Islander Commission
CEO	Chief Executive Officer
COAG	Council of Australian Governments
CRA	Conzinc Riotinto of Australia Ltd
EHSIS	Environmental Heritage and Social Impact Services
ILC	Indigenous Land Corporation
ILUA	Indigenous Land Use Agreement
KALACC	Kimberley Aboriginal Law and Culture Centre
KAPCO	Kimberley Agriculture and Pastoral Company
KLC	Kimberley Land Council
KRED	KRED Enterprises
LNG	liquified natural gas
NDT	Northern Development Taskforce
NNTT	National Native Title Tribunal
NSW	New South Wales
PBC	Prescribed Body Corporate
PTTEP Australasia	a subsidiary of PTT Exploration and Production Public Company Limited (PTTEP), the Thai national petroleum exploration and production company
WA	Western Australia / Western Australian

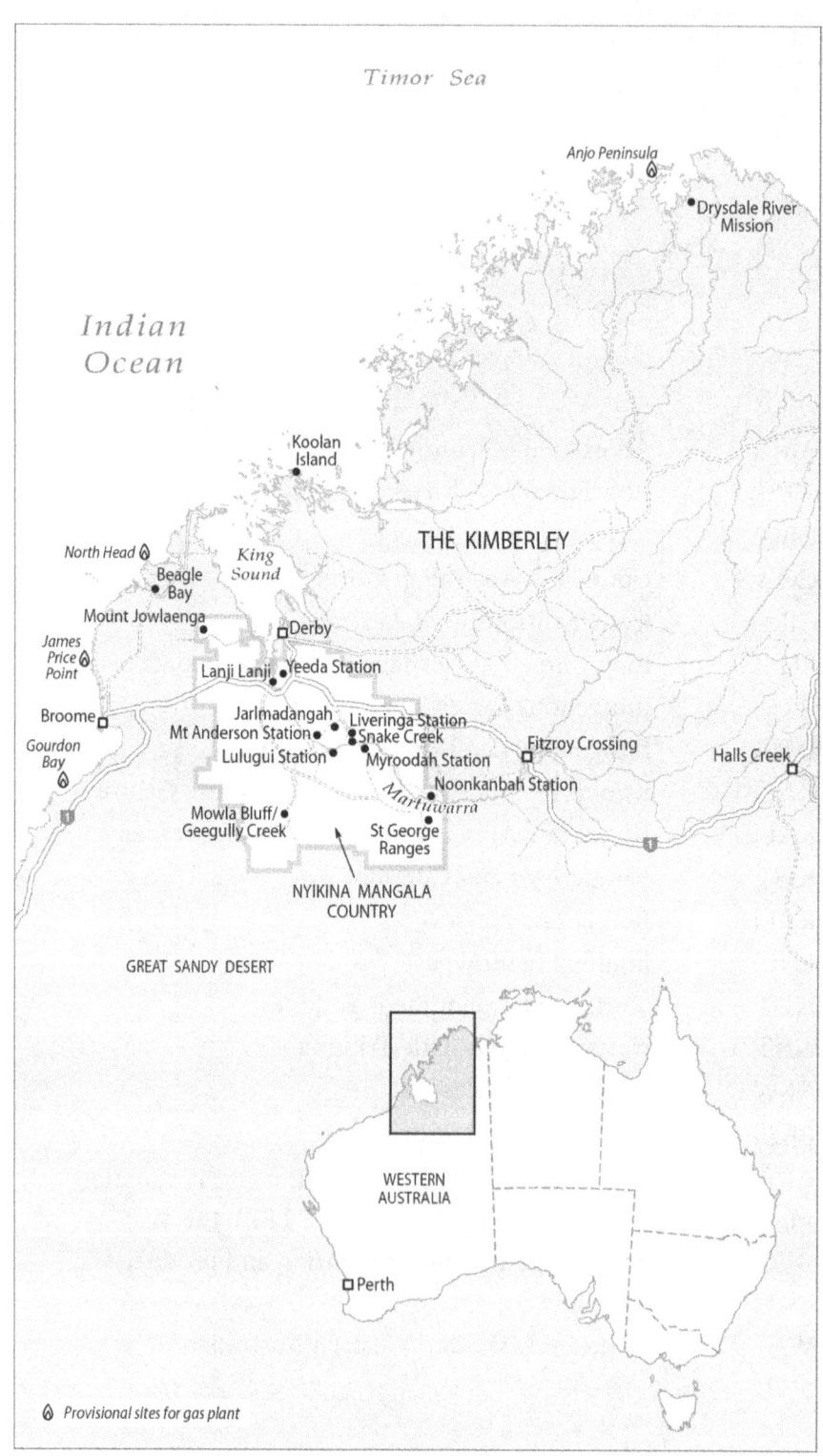

The Kimberley

Prologue: Bilby killer

'Your dad kills baby bilbies.'

This is what they say to his children.

'You think white. You lie white. You talk white.'

This is what they say to him.

A Ku Klux Klan hat and a hangman's noose swing from a lamp-post on the road into town.

This is what they say to the people of Broome, a place in the Kimberley region of Western Australia that prides itself on its Aboriginal and Asian history. A multicultural town. A welcoming town.

There comes a breaking point.

For Nyikina man Wayne Bergmann, that point is in August 2011.

Earlier in the year, he'd stepped down as chief executive of one of the most powerful land councils in Australia—the Kimberley Land Council (KLC). After exhaustive consultations with native title groups, Wayne had successfully negotiated a 1.5 billion dollar compensation agreement between the Western Australian Government, Woodside Petroleum Ltd and Kimberley Traditional Owners over a proposed gas plant at James Price Point, just north of Broome.

The proposal ripped the town right up the belly.

It turned brothers against sisters, daughters against fathers, employees against bosses, friends against friends. There was no sitting on the fence. You were either for or against a gas plant.

'Dad, why can't you do a job where people like you?' asked his daughter Tessa.

Tessa was still too young to know that native title gives no veto over development.[1] That if you refuse a seat at the table, you might end up with nothing. That for Aboriginal people facing development proposals, there is no level playing field. That the economic rights of her ancestors had long since been taken away.

By August, Wayne is exhausted. His children have been bullied at school—even his eldest daughter, Sara, who's boarding two thousand kilometres south, in Perth. His wife, Christine, has been abused while grocery shopping. For the last eight years, he's been trying to hold Kimberley Traditional Owners together. For eight years, he's been fighting the Australian Government, the Western Australian Government, the pastoralists, the media and the protesters. He's been fighting Woodside—is fighting them right at this moment, urging the company to release sensitive footage to the public showing non-Aboriginal protesters spitting on Aboriginal people employed to conduct heritage clearances at the proposed site.

'We live here,' he tells Woodside staff in a meeting in Broome. 'We're being attacked every day. You need to tell the truth about what's happening.'

But Woodside won't budge. Won't make the footage public.

It's the first time Wayne loses control in his professional career. He thumps the table with his fist and walks out of the meeting in tears. He feels broken; they've broken him. Wayne drives home, packs the car, and then keeps driving, with Christine in the front and their two youngest children, Jarred and Tessa, in the back.

They pass the crocodile park and the mango farms of 12 Mile. They skirt portly old boabs and cross floodplains of whistling ducks. Finally, they draw close to the mighty Martuwarra, the Fitzroy River—lifeblood of Nyikina country, Wayne's country, his children's country—made by Woonyoomboo when the world was still soft.

1: With rosaries in one hand, revolvers in the other

Senior Nyikina woman Annie Milgin says Woonyoomboo was a botanist, a cartographer, a scientist and a doctor. He travelled the length and breadth of Nyikina country leaving stories, songs, marks, and meeting many people who would turn into the creatures that live on country today (Milgin and Thompson). When, at the end of his journey, Woonyoomboo became a night heron, he tasked the spirit people and the Nyikina people to look after country. For tens of thousands of years the Nyikina followed Woonyoomboo's instructions. They used madjala, a freshwater mangrove, as both a medicine and to draw oxygen from the water to make it easier to catch fish; they obeyed strict rules around skin groups, which determined tribal responsibilities and relationships; and they kept their language, law, culture and clan groupings strong.

But things radically changed with the arrival of white settlers.

In 1880, Hamlet Cornish, from Pinjarra, south of Perth, was inspired to follow in the footsteps of government explorer and surveyor Alexander Forrest, who had come across a 'magnificent' and 'beautifully grassed' pastoral land in the state's north (Forrest 4–6). The young man's goal was to set up a sheep station with the Murray Squatting Company. As he scoured Nyikina country for a suitable location, he encountered the world created by Woonyoomboo, a world of brackish billabongs, scented acacias and plentiful game—two bullets were enough to kill fifty ducks for dinner. He observed graves, bark-bound corpses laid carefully on platforms in the trees and visited a cave of exquisite art. He was surprised to discover the 'wild savages' had such instinct (Cornish 9). The area was densely populated, and Cornish and his party could see twists of smoke from Nyikina campfires in every direction. But, despite shimmers of curiosity about their culture, Cornish became increasingly suspicious and fearful of the local people, who he described as 'cheeky', 'troublesome' and 'too familiar' (Cornish 10, 12).

The feeling was mutual.

The Nyikina were wary of these men who looked like ghosts, wary of their weapons. One evening, a group of men threw their spears into the packs of Cornish's party—perhaps mistaking the packs for the sleeping bodies of the settlers. With nerves on edge, Cornish responded in the coming days by scattering any curious locals with bullets. In his diaries, the reasons for provocation are unclear. Was it simply a case of the Nyikina protecting their country? Or had Cornish's party made other transgressions? In the decades to come, sexual abuse and domestic use of Aboriginal women was found to be the primary cause of attacks on settlers and their property.

What is clear is that by the time Cornish chose a site for Yeeda Station—traditionally Yuluwaja—he was convinced the 'natives' were plotting to murder them all.

The first casualty on the settlers' side was Neah from Perth's Swan River, one of three Aboriginal men in Cornish's party. He was found on a claypan with his skull smashed to pulp, a spear jammed down his throat and another spear through his back. His hair had been hacked off and his arms and legs broken. This was an Aboriginal tradition to stop any spirits coming back to haunt the assaulters.

The next casualty was Cornish's brother, Anthony 'Tony' Cornish. Tony had travelled north in 1882 as a representative of the settler-owned Kimberley Pastoral Company. He'd swiftly selected a site for a homestead not far from Yeeda on a tributary of the Fitzroy and this became Lulugui Station. Its Nyikina name is Kulakulaku. One morning, Tony left the station for an outer camp to set up some new yards. It was the heart of the wet season, a time when the river swelled dark with snags, and the black soil was deep enough to drown sheep. The group hadn't travelled far when Tony realised he'd forgotten his pencil and paper. He left his axe with a local man, Guirella, and cantered back to the homestead, a large hat drawn low to shade his eyes.[2]

When he returned, he didn't ask for his axe back.

A little further along the track Tony dismissed several members of the group. He was now alone with Guirella, and Guirella's wife, Neuri. Upon reaching an old camp, the sheep fanned out and became difficult to drive. Perhaps leveraging Tony's inattention, Guirella screamed at his wife to *run*!

Tony turned to watch the woman.

Moments later, he buckled from his horse.

Tony's body was found in a pool of blood and mud, with split skull, oblique gashes to the neck, and a spear hole in the right breast. He was the first white settler recorded killed in the Kimberley.

In Cornish's diary, in the breaths between sentences, there are omissions, possibilities, questions. Why had Tony dismissed the other members of the group? Was he planning on doing something he didn't want them to see? Why did Guirella urge his wife to run? Who else might have been watching from the spaces between trees?

Wayne Bergmann's great-great-grandmother, Lucy Muninga, was in her early teens.

She would have known Guirella and Neuri.

She would have been appalled by what happened next.

Hamlet Cornish and his party—devastated by Tony's death—swore 'vengeance against the niggers' (Cornish 17). They followed the marshy bends of the Martuwarra, strode across pindan and offered two local Aboriginal men a bag of flour for Guirella's head. A couple of weeks into their hunt they stormed a camp, locking several old warriors in neck chains and proceeding to chain up everyone who arrived at the camp that afternoon. By evening, they held forty men and women captive. The air was sharp with urine, sour with fear. The men and women cried, writhed. Their chains tangled. Cornish used a small sharp file to break the links, untangling them, then put the prisoners on fresh chains, taking 'every precaution to make them behave themselves in the future' (Cornish 18).

The captives were released upon the seizure of Guirella and Neuri. The couple were hauled aboard a government cutter, the *Gertrude*, where Guirella was tried for wilful murder and sent to an all-white jury trial in Perth. A Mr Horgan was appointed as Guirella's lawyer. Horgan objected to Neuri giving evidence—wives couldn't be forced to give evidence against their husbands at the time. But the judge overturned the objection, saying he didn't recognise the couple to be husband and wife. Horgan also protested that one of the interpreters, Samuel Elliott, was too close to the case, a partner of Cornish's from Yeeda. But the judge didn't take issue with this either, and Elliott was permitted to interpret along with a Fitzroy local.

Neuri said she'd fled. She'd heard Tony shout but hadn't seen what happened. When Guirella caught up with her, he was carrying the axe, wet with blood, and he said he'd killed the pastoralist.

Neuri had no idea these words, relayed through the interpreters, would be her husband's death knell.

Guirella's story was different. He said Tony Cornish had given him a letter to take to a station about a mile and a half away. When he came back, the white man was dead.

What may have been lost in the space between languages, in the chasm between laws?

On 18 June 1883, Guirella was hanged offshore from Perth at Wadjemup, Rottnest Island, known by Noongar people as the 'place where spirits come to rest' (Wynne). At the time of Guirella's incarceration, the island had become a place of restless spirits, not rested spirits. The white settlers were referring to it as a 'fever-den from which few blacks ever return' ('The West Australian Nigger' 40).

* * *

The following decades saw a deadly measles epidemic sweep forty miles up the Martuwarra, a scorching drought shrink native food sources, and a white colonist declare in the *Eastern Districts Chronicle* that 'one man with a reliable revolver on a good horse could disperse a whole tribe [along the Fitzroy River] as long as it was light' ('Minnie-Pool Charley' 2).

'Disperse' was a standard euphemism for murder.

In 1893, Alexander Forrest, now a politician with significant pastoral interests in the Kimberley, asked parliament whether 'the life of one European is not worth a thousand natives, so far as the settlement of the country is concerned'. He described the hill tribes as 'utterly useless. You can do nothing with them, and they won't have anything to do with the whites, except to spear their sheep and cattle ... I have seen them myself, on the top of a hill 2,000ft.

high, rolling stones down upon you' (Forrest, Western Australian Parliamentary 1052).

Aboriginal people who threatened white settlement, who retaliated after their women had been taken, who speared livestock after their native food sources had been depleted, found themselves the target of attacks from police and pastoralists.

Perhaps it was fear that motivated Wayne's great-great-grandmother Muninga to seek work on Yeeda. For her services she likely received flour, sugar, tea, tobacco, food and basic clothing; this idea of reciprocity was grounded in her cultural upbringing. What was perhaps less widely understood by Aboriginal pastoral workers was that their indenture to station owners sometimes made them prisoners on their own land. If they absconded, they could be arrested and returned to the station; if they disobeyed their 'master's lawful commands', they could be jailed (Owen, 280–281).

The threat of jail also hung over those alleged to have speared livestock. In many instances, the men arrested for spearing livestock were not guilty. Accompanied by 'witnesses' to the alleged crime, the men were walked to jail in neck chains. Witnesses were usually young women who were raped at night: first by the police, then by the assisting stockmen, and finally by the Aboriginal trackers. The police received blood money—payment per head for the number of prisoners and witnesses they brought in. One jailer admitted that of twenty Aboriginal people in his charge sentenced for cattle killing, not one understood why he'd been arrested (*Royal* 20).

In 1905 the *Aborigines Act* was passed, giving the state almost complete control over Aboriginal people's lives. A Chief Protector became the legal guardian of all Aboriginal and 'half-caste' children under the age of sixteen, people's movements were restricted, and children under the age of sixteen could be rounded up, removed and sent to missions. This was justified by James Isdell, Travelling Inspector and Protector of Aborigines in the Kimberley, who commented: 'The half-caste is intellectually above the aborigine, and it is the duty of the State that they be given a chance to lead a better life than their mothers. I would not hesitate for one moment to separate any half-caste from its aboriginal mother, no matter how frantic her momentary grief might be at the time. They soon forget their offspring' (Isdell 9, 1909 report).

Wayne's great-great-grandmother Muninga never forgot her baby daughter. Her daughter's Aboriginal name was Jira, anglicised as Sarah Phillipina Melycan. Jira was born on Yeeda Station to an Indian father, Jimmy Cassim. By the age of seven she was living in Derby, where her mum washed and ironed for the Chinese-Australian Quan Sing family. One cool morning in 1908, Jira was playing outside Quan Sing's house with her cousin-sister Gypsy, and a little boy named Albert.[3] A police buggy and horse appeared. It slowed as it neared the children. Two Aboriginal police boys sang out to them in Nyikina. *Do you want to go for a ride?* Albert fled, but the two girls jumped in. They were taken straight to the old Derby jail.

The jail was more of a cage than a building, with iron grilles for walls and a concrete slab for a floor. Sixteen ring bolts were set into the concrete, to which prisoners were fastened with chains. As dusk settled, the girls huddled closer together. It was just the two of them. Why were they here? Why couldn't they get out? Why wouldn't their mum help them? They could hear her but couldn't see her.

All night, Muninga wailed for them in language.

The next morning the girls were ushered onto a tram which would take them out to the jetty. As they passed their mother, the police held on to their wrists so tightly it hurt. 'Mum!' they cried.

Muninga was beating her forehead the traditional way, to express her grief, her sorrow; her face was bright with rivulets of blood.

'Mum!'

But there was no time to stop, no time to talk, no time to say goodbye.

The girls, bawling their eyes out, were whisked onto a waiting ship bound for the mission at Beagle Bay.

* * *

Wayne's great-grandfather Yoolya was born on Nyikina country in the shadow of a windmill at Snake Creek. Yoolya's mother, Wadadarl Brumby, worked on Liveringa and Myroodah stations. His father was Liveringa's third manager, Percy Rose, and his legal guardian was a Scotsman, Walter Fraser. In 1909, a year after Muninga lost her daughter to the mission, Yoolya, too, drew the attention of the authorities.

Kimberley Protector James Isdell was on a hunt for half-caste children. For over a month he travelled by foot and mule cart along the Fitzroy River. It was a throttling forty-three degrees in the shade, and of the children he captured, two fell ill. Others absconded. Yoolya was among those successfully transported to Derby. From Derby, the eleven-year-old was ushered aboard the steamship *Koombana* along with seven other boys. The boys were dumped at the Drysdale River Mission at Pago, on the north Kimberley coast.

Pago was so remote a boat might stop by only once every six months.

The mission was on the lands of the Kwini people—coastal sandplain country shaded by woolly butts and stringybarks.[4] It had only been operational since the year before and was run by

Spanish Benedictine monks whose goal was 'the conversion of the wild aborigines' (Torres 135). The missionaries were dismayed by the treatment of Kimberley Aboriginal people, observing, 'Too frequently they are shamelessly ill-used by Europeans, who deprive them of their land and most inhumanely murder them' (Perez 2). At Pago they constructed a sanctuary of sorts, with a monastery, a well and extensive gardens. Yoolya was put to work tending coconut trees, mangoes, watermelons and peanuts. He was taught carpentry and blacksmithing, learned English and Spanish. The monks didn't call him by his Aboriginal name; in 1910 Yoolya was baptised Fulgentius, after the Abbot of New Norcia, Fulgentius Torres. Later in life he would also be known as Fred Fraser.

Relations between the missionaries and local Aboriginal people were strained. During an early encounter, the missionaries abducted and detained a woman, resulting in a fierce retaliation by local men. After this, the monks lived in constant fear of further attacks. They prayed with rosaries in one hand, revolvers in the other. When the sun dipped, they would climb to the second storey of their monastery and withdraw the ladder before they slept.

In September 1913, 103 local Aboriginal people were lured to the mission by the promise of freshly cut watermelon. While the monks were distributing the fruit, someone gave a signal and the local men picked up their weapons. Father Alcalde was 'speared through and pinned to the ground' and Father Altimira was bashed with an *ualo*, a club, and was also wounded by a spear (Perez 20).

Yoolya watched the escalating violence from behind the garden fence. The monks were like family. He had to act—had to protect them. So he raced to the mission house and grabbed a gun. He'd never touched a gun and it was heavy in his hands. He ran back out and fired a shot above the heads of the men and women. They fled. No lives were lost—at least not straight away. Many years later, Father Alcalde would die in Perth from the injuries he suffered that day.

After the event, the missionaries found that the local people 'were unable to give an explanation for this their treacherous behaviour' (Perez 32). But an Aboriginal oral history revealed a possible reason for the attack. The missionaries had shot dead a dog belonging to one of the men. It was a good dog, a kangaroo-hunting dog, and the attack may have been payback.

There were further incidents, too. When a British company established a pastoral station nearby at Narrin, on the banks of the Drysdale River, the local people fiercely defended their country from the invaders. In a manner which was strategic, calculated and deliberate, they killed a third of the station's stock, not only for food, but to sabotage the pastoralists' business. Cattle were trampling their cultural sites, fouling their water places. Their resistance was so persistent they pushed the pastoralists out. One old man, who has now passed away, said, 'The old people gave the whitefellas such a hard time that they gave up and left' (Crawford 168).

*　*　*

Back on Nyikina country, the whitefellas hadn't given up, nor had they left. In fact, they kept coming, transiting through Derby in pursuit of pearls, land, wealth, even bones …

In 1910, Eric Mjöberg, a Swedish ethnographer and zoologist, arrived in Derby wearing a tropical pith helmet and a pair of white pants. The non-Aboriginal people the Swede encountered were permanently tired; they languished like convalescents in wicker chairs and always seemed to be leaning against railings or door frames. But Mjöberg refused to be defeated by heat. He was on a mission to possess specimens.

Mjöberg set off from Derby on 11 October with a team of bullocks, an ornithologist, a taxidermist, a fellow ethnographer and several others who would leave before the ten-month expedition was complete. In his work, he was methodical, observant, predatory: a pale-grey mantis felt the clamp of his tweezers around her waist; hundreds of red-and-black beetles were ushered into a cyanide jar; an entire bowerbird nest was uprooted and placed in a sack.

Mjöberg considered the Aboriginal people he encountered to be 'cunning and devious' as well as 'suspicious and superstitious' (Mjöberg 142–43). Those working on stations were 'lazy, degenerate remnants' and 'half-parasitic' (Mjöberg 197). Yet he was reliant on Nyikina men as his guides. On the way to Mount Anderson Station he camped close to a boab tree which had been inscribed with an arrow and the words 'to Hell'. Further along, in the homestead of Noonkanbah Station, he noted the white men lived in a disarray of dirty blankets, spurs, sooty pots and house-dwelling chickens. In the St George Ranges he found the fresh tracks of an Aboriginal child and speculated that it might be interesting to capture the child and hold him hostage. While resting at a freshwater spring unmarked on any settlers' map, one of his Aboriginal guides told him the spring was home to a spirit who reigns over rain. Mjöberg promptly named the site after his son.

In addition to collecting animal embryos, skins, and brains, Mjöberg also sought to acquire ethnographic material. He stole weapons, ornaments, tools, toys, sandals made of plant fibre, and sculptures strictly relating to men's business. Most horrifying was his theft of six human skeletons and several human skulls.

Like Hamlet Cornish before him, Mjöberg observed human

bodies resting on platforms in the trees. He ransacked one tree-grave by using his pocketknife to pry loose the bones. Shortly afterward he travelled to a place referred to as Skeleton Hill, where he encountered natural crypts: caves filled with ancient bones wrapped in paperbark. Here he stole skulls. On the way back to his main camp he needed to ford a river and so disguised the bones in three large sacks and sought help from some Aboriginal men working on a nearby station. He gave the men tobacco and told them the sacks contained the nests of birds and the skeletons of kangaroos. He writes, 'Inwardly I laughed, at the three Negroes happily chatting [as they] walked ahead of me carrying the remains of their dead comrades' (Mjöberg 179).

Mjöberg lied to customs officials in Fremantle so he could smuggle the skeletons home to Sweden. As the ship finally left Australia, he mused that the country was the 'earth's largest and most interesting open-air museum' (Mjöberg 327). The 'museum' would eventually haunt him to death. On return to Sweden, he fell ill with a long and undiagnosable sickness. He was tortured by nightmares—Aboriginal people hunted him, relentlessly, and he was pursued by spirits from the Dreamtime.

Eighty-three years after Mjöberg's expedition, when Wayne Bergmann became the head of the Kimberley Aboriginal Law and Culture Centre (KALACC), one of his first jobs was the repatriation of sacred materials. KALACC continued to pursue this work actively in the following decades and, in 2004, with the help of Mjöberg's great-niece, the stolen skeletons were finally returned to Nyikina country and laid to rest.

* * *

While Mjöberg tramped across Nyikina country, Wayne's great-grandmother Jira was adjusting to life at the Beagle Bay Mission, north of Broome, on the traditional lands of the Nyul Nyul people. Over a hundred children lived on the mission and at times there were as many as two hundred local Aboriginal people on site—particularly when food was scarce. Among the young women there were those like Jira, who had been stolen from their mothers. There were also the 'prostitutes', women who'd had liaisons with Asian or European men, and the mission was a haven for the elderly, the sick and for people with disabilities.

The Beagle Bay complex consisted of over twenty buildings. Girls were housed in one dormitory, boys in another. There were classrooms, dining rooms, a slaughter yard and cattle. The gardens yielded oranges, bananas and dates; the fields produced sorghum and haricot beans. On a visit in 1908, Kimberley Protector James Isdell wrote of the prodigious freshwater springs. 'In the shade of the cocoanut [sic] trees is a deep plunge bath in the centre of a large spring, the water always icy cold' (Isdell 20, 1908 report).

This was the world Jira awoke to at 6.15 every morning. Rubbing sleep from her eyes, she would rise from her stretcher and attend church. After church, she had breakfast, then school: first inside a classroom, and later, when the heat became too oppressive, under a tree. When school was finished for the day Jira worked in the sewing room or the kitchen or the laundry. She was being trained as a domestic servant. Aboriginal girls were cheaper to employ than European people with similar skills.

In 1918, the monks at Drysdale River Mission sent Yoolya to Beagle Bay to find a wife. He worked on the mission as a baker and soon began to court Jira. The two married and went on to have eight children—seven girls and a boy.

Their second child, Aggie, was Wayne's grandmother.

Nana Aggie remembers meeting her grandmother, Muninga, just the once.

A letter had arrived for Jira, stating that Muninga was in Broome. Nana Aggie remembers the priest saying, *'Look ... there's a truck going in tomorrow, you can take all the children, they can go with you to see your mother.* And we all went to Broome. We had to walk four miles to where they were camping. In those days, there was no transport. Well, it was nothing to us. So, we walked right across the plain and when we looked, we could see this—we said, *Who this woman there, getting herself all worked up?* We could see it. We didn't understand the meaning of it. She started getting this stick and started to flog herself with it. When she seen her daughter, she made her daughter out. Mum (Jira) must have had that thing with her mother straight away, she knew that was her mother. That was the biggest rejoicing of Mum, for Mum to meet her mother, when she had five of us. I never seen her no more after that. She died. That was the last' (Puertollano).

Wayne's various family members reflected on the mission days with conflicting feelings. His great-aunts remembered the nuns eating all the good food and the children just getting the leftovers. They felt they had missed out on having a mother, missed out on learning how to develop proper family relationships. Yet other family members had an enduring respect toward their surrogate parents. Yoolya, after he'd finished a droving job at Meekatharra in the Mid West, travelled a further 650 kilometres south on horseback to visit his old mentor and friend Father Alcalde. He rode across deserts and skirted the salt-white edges of ancient lakes. Upon reaching the New Norcia Mission, Yoolya was warmly received and the two men spent long hours in conversation. A later report in the

St Ildephonsus College Magazine described his 'courteous bearing', 'eagerness to learn' and 'stout, brave heart' (Benedictine Community 43). When he received a telegram from his employer requesting that he get back to work, Yoolya packed without complaint and set off that same evening.

Wayne's grandmother, Nana Aggie, also held fond memories of her mission upbringing. She was born at Drysdale River Mission and had grown up at Beagle Bay. Wayne remembers her saying things like, 'You can't talk bad about the nuns. They were our mothers!' Aggie was grateful for the education she received, and proud of her work—proud to tell her grandchildren that she'd been a domestic at the magistrate's house in Broome. She also believed her family was safer on the mission, out of the direct control of the government.

She may have been right.

Aboriginal men and women who still lived on country were often in grave danger. In 1916, when Aggie's mum, Jira, was at Beagle Bay, and her dad, Yoolya, was at Drysdale, an expedition of police and pastoralists set out across Nyikina and then Mangala country to punish a man whose dog had killed a sheep.[5] The expedition was led by a Mangala man called Gunna, who was thirsty for revenge against his own people. He led the police and pastoralists to a group of around four hundred Mangala, Nyikina and Karajarri people at Geegully Creek, then tricked the people into collecting wood for a giant fire. As soon as the fire blazed hot, the police and pastoralists shot dead the adults. They didn't single out the man whose dog had killed a sheep—they murdered everyone. Children and babies were whacked across the head to save bullets. All of the bodies were dragged into the fire. But the evidence didn't vanish, not completely.

Senior Nyikina man John Darraga Watson was taken to the massacre site in 1959 and saw bits of bone, saw the soil was still black from the fat of the people who had been burned. He writes, 'Some kartiya [non-Aboriginal] historians accuse us of making up these stories and say we can't prove it. But our old people couldn't write down their stories... we know they put some of these bad bastards onto our old people, and that's how they put us down, how they cut us out from country' (Watson 60).

* * *

In the 1920s an Englishman, Harold Godbehear, encountered a vital and violent landscape in north-west WA—a place where sheep were sometimes mustered with camels, Afghans still fought with knives, and a white stockman might shoot the genitals from his white wife's Aboriginal lover. Godbehear settled on Myroodah Station, or Kakinpala. He became the station's part-owner and manager and spent the next thirty-eight years on Nyikina country.

Godbehear's first memory of the station was of the ginger-haired cook chasing 'his gin' around the meat house with a cleaver.[6] He then went on to observe the homestead, which was ravaged by white ants and dry rot, and noted the only buildings of consequence were the shearing sheds and the store. While the station was somewhat shabby, Godbehear found the surrounding country bewitching. In his journals he describes the 'cathedral-like arch of those white towering gums' at Myroodah Crossing, the river holes filled with barramundi, sharks, sawfish and stingrays, and the 'utter grandeur' of the sunsets (Godbehear 37–59).

Godbehear's life soon fell into pace with the seasons. With the approach of the wet, he sensed a suppressed excitement amongst his seventy-odd Aboriginal workers. Before leaving for six weeks of ceremonies (which would take place on a law ground within the station's boundaries), the workers were issued with food, tobacco and fabric for loincloths. This time off allowed people to keep their language, law and culture strong.

Once the wet season set in, Myroodah became cut off from Derby, the closest town. Godbehear quotes an old rover who, when describing the wet to people down south, would say, 'It rains and rains and rains; dead donkeys twenty feet in the trees …' (Godbehear 37). When the Martuwarra had fallen again, its level could be measured by the flood marks on the timber.

One of Godbehear's most vivid memories was of a tribal murder—the prime suspect was one of his stockmen. The police visited the station and, believing the body to be entombed in a termite mound, proceeded to demolish three of them. The suspect looked on, bored, chewing tobacco, pointing with his chin and saying 'might be that one' (Godbehear 64).

They never found the body and the tribal killing went unsolved.

Godbehear's nostalgia-tinged recollections of station life, penned long after he'd left the Kimberley for a cooler retirement in Perth, are tempered by Aboriginal oral histories. For decades, the majority of stockmen in the Kimberley were Aboriginal and they worked hard and without wages: fencing, branding, horning, spaying and droving. The women often undertook the same jobs as the men, as well as cooking, collecting water and cleaning for their white bosses. Some of the bosses were real savages. Barney Barnes, a Walmajarri man who worked on Christmas Creek Station, recalled a little boy who was shot dead by the station's cook. The boy's body was burned in front of all the staff—including women and children. When they began to weep, the manager hollered, 'Shut up before I blow you buggers out!' (Watson et al. 258).

Godbehear didn't have the cruel streak of some of the other

pastoralists in the region, but Lochy Green, a Mangala man who worked for a time on Myroodah, remembered how sometimes, when people were very sick, Godbehear would say it was too late to take them to the hospital and that he couldn't spare anyone to accompany them. 'We used to lose some of our old people on the station that way. They used to die,' he reflected (Watson et al. 187).

Wayne's great-grandfather Yoolya, however, had a relationship of mutual respect with Godbehear. He had earned a reputation as a trustworthy and hard worker—after leaving the mission, he was employed for ten years with the Broome-based pastoral and pearling enterprise Streeter and Male, and he'd also worked at Ethel Creek Station in the Pilbara. At Myroodah, Godbehear put him in charge of the bottom sheep camp and paid him a wage. While Yoolya enjoyed his work, he was conscious that he was regarded as a second-class citizen. In 1936, when the *Native Administration Act* amended the earlier *Aborigines Act 1905*, it gave the government even further control over Aboriginal people.

With Godbehear's assistance, Yoolya applied for an exemption from the Act for himself and his family. This was significant because it meant the family would receive citizenship certificates and would have the same rights as white Australians. It also meant the family had to live according to white standards and could not mingle with other Aboriginal people or visit Aboriginal camps. Should they breach these conditions, their citizenship could be withdrawn. The certificates were referred to widely as 'dog tags' or 'dog licences'.

Godbehear provided the following written reference: 'This man is generally spoken well of by those [who] have employed him which reports I can fully endorse … Fraser [Yoolya] is in a position of trust and responsibility and I would be most grateful for anything you may be good enough to do in this matter on his behalf.' When the bureaucratic process stalled, Godbehear followed up with a letter to the Commissioner of Native Affairs. 'You may remember my call upon you when in Perth some time ago in regard to a half-caste here named Fraser who is applying to be "made a white man." He has recently written to you again ...' (Native Affairs)

Exemption was finally granted in March 1941—though only to Yoolya, Sarah Phillipina (Jira) and their children under fourteen. Their daughter Aggie, Wayne's grandmother, applied later for herself. One of the perks of citizenship was being able to drink at the pub alongside non-Aboriginal Australians. In later years, when the family had moved to Derby, Aggie was known to storm down to the Spinifex Hotel and haul Yoolya out with a firm 'Dad! I think you've had enough!'. She wasn't afraid to growl someone who deserved a dressing down—be it the priest, the police, or the school principal. Even as a very young woman, Wayne's grandmother Aggie wouldn't take nonsense from anyone.

At around the age of sixteen she worked as a cook on Myroodah Station for the stockmen under the sharp eye of Godbehear's wife. Aggie's sister, Frances, also worked in the homestead as a housekeeper. The girls were paid ten shillings and five shillings a week respectively ('Shoulder to Shoulder' 8). Mrs Godbehear had a reputation—she could be a tough and nasty boss. One day Aggie snapped. She tossed a bowl of flour over Mrs Godbehear's head and bolted from the homestead with her sister. The girls didn't flee via the road, where they could be easily tracked, but through the spinifex.

Godbehear chased them, and he got close—so close the girls had to crouch quietly in the thorny shade of a conkerberry tree.

'Any tracks?' Mr Godbehear asked the Aboriginal station hand accompanying him.

'No. No, boss,' the station hand replied. 'No tracks.'

When the two men finally turned around, the girls continued—softly, cautiously, until they reached their dad, who was working at the bottom sheep camp. Yoolya urged them to return to the station, but Aggie—too headstrong, too stubborn—initially refused.

Wayne remembers hearing this story from his grandmother when he was a child.

Aggie went on to marry young Thomas Puertollano, who had a Filipino father and an Aboriginal Nyul Nyul mother. He had also grown up at the Beagle Bay Mission. Together they had three children, Cyril, Patricia and Shirley—Patricia would become Wayne's mum.

* * *

When Wayne reflects on his family history, on the bruising impacts of colonisation, he wonders at the exact nature of those first encounters. He wonders if there was a degree of curiosity and cordiality between the two groups—as suggested in Alexander Forrest's diaries chronicling the early exploration of the area. If there was, any goodwill was swiftly superseded by suspicion, then hostility, when the settlers moved in for good. The attacks on the settlers were not simply skirmishes—episodes of unpremeditated fighting. They were deliberate, provoked, and prompted by a desire to protect Nyikina country and women.

As a young fella, Wayne 'had a romantic view' of his family's contributions to the Kimberley pastoral industry. 'I grew up believing that if you were a good, hard worker then you were a quality person. As I got older, and started working on stations myself, I learned this wasn't always the case. I would sit in amongst the white station workers—hard workers, but rednecks—and they'd say, even to the older Aboriginal men, *Hey boy. Hey boy, come here and do this.* You'd have the Aboriginal quarters, then the kartiya [non-Aboriginal] quarters. There was still segregation.'

The world Wayne was born into was one where the legacy of Forrest, the Cornish brothers, Mjöberg, the Beagle Bay nuns and the Benedictine monks was still felt acutely. It was a world where frontier massacres had occurred within living memory. And it was a world where justice, under whitefella law, didn't often grace Kimberley Aboriginal people.

In 2018 Wayne mused, 'When you reflect on these things, the dominant society was always trying to get Aboriginal people to think small and be small. It's a reflection of power and control. It's never been about justice' (Fox 74). Wayne—with an approach that was single-minded, relentless and sometimes ruthless—would recast his world and upend the status quo. He would take on pastoralists, mining companies and governments, all of whom had had their fingers pressed to the spines of his people for over a century.

2: The shadows that don't exist

On a warm winter's day in 1969, Patricia Mary Puertollano gave birth to her third child, a baby boy with blond locks. It was 27 June, the season of Wilbooroo: a time for crocodile eggs and bush orange blossoms. Pat was twenty-three years old and her new baby, Wayne Thomas Puertollano, quickly became the talk of the neighbourhood—the girls adored his hair, the gossipers wondered who the father was.

Wayne grew up between his mum's home and his Nana Aggie's home. When he was a young boy, Nana Aggie would take him fishing in King Sound, an immense body of water that surged with whirlpools, crocodiles and the stiff, dead limbs of trees. King Sound has one of the biggest tidal ranges in the world. On a spring low, they would walk across the exposed sandbars and mud flats to fish one of Aggie's secret crevices. She would sing out, 'Old people, we're here, fishing, bring us luck!' and she would gift a handful of sand to the water to let country know she was there. Aggie would always leave her line out until the very last minute—until they could hear the thunder of the incoming tide. Then, with her cast net and fish under one arm, and Wayne under the other, she'd dash back to the Derby jetty, chased by thick tongues of mud.

Aggie was legendary for her generosity. If she came home with ten barramundi, she'd give half of them away. She often cooked up a big mob of fish, curry, rice and damper and shared it among families and the other people in the neighbourhood. This impulse to help people, to give back to her community, was grounded in both her Catholic and cultural values.

When Wayne wasn't with Nana Aggie or his Uncle Cyril, he was playing with, or tormenting, his two older sisters, Helen and Angela. Sometimes he would chase the girls around the backyard with a spear. Once Wayne doused Helen with boiling water; another time he cut her wrists with a breadknife.

Wayne believes these actions were in response to the violence around him. His mum, Pat, had a boyfriend called Billy Dubbo. Dubbo was a Thursday Islander, a bloke who, Pat says, 'didn't talk but hit … who smashed plates and would often come home drunk'.

One of Wayne's most distinct childhood memories is of racing toward the sound of his mum screaming. Pat was pinned to the lino at the foot of the old stove. Dubbo was sitting on her stomach, belting her. His fist cracked against her chin, her cheek, thudded into her breasts. Wayne remembers picking up a knife, not a breadknife this time but a butcher's knife, razor-sharp, with a heavy wooden handle. Dubbo paused, turned, and goaded the seven-year-old, 'Go on, you just try.' Wayne hesitated, knowing he had to help his mum but worrying he'd be in big strife if he killed his mum's boyfriend.

He dropped the knife.

Dubbo climbed off her and not long afterwards disappeared from their lives all together.

Wayne also recalls that more broadly, within the community, there wasn't just physical violence, but sexual violence too, particularly against children. 'It was something people didn't talk about,' Wayne says. 'To this day, it's unacknowledged and unconfronted. You can't confront it, can't even shadow-box it, if the shadows don't exist.'

* * *

Pat had fallen in love with other blokes prior to Billy Dubbo. Before the girls and Wayne came along, she'd quit her job at the welfare office in Derby and hightailed it to Darwin, where she worked as a cleaner and rode around on a fancy Italian Lambretta. Here she met Aeneas Menus, a Greek, who became Angela and Helen's dad. Aeneas left Darwin for an arranged marriage in Greece and was never heard from again. Pat then hooked up with his best friend, Johnny Skiadas, also a Greek, who would become Wayne's biological father. Johnny's still alive and living in Perth, but Wayne has little to do with him.

By the time Bradley was born, Pat was bringing up three young children as a single mum. Wayne recalls, 'Mum had been incredible growing us three kids up. At different times she held jobs babysitting, cleaning, ironing clothes and packing meat. But when Bradley came along, she felt ashamed by the prospect of having to go before the court to justify another child payment. He was only a year younger than me, and there was pressure from the church. The church organised for Pat to have the baby in Perth. After Bradley was born, he was to be given up for adoption. But when mum held Bradley in her arms, she changed her mind. *I want to keep him*, she told the hospital staff. But they insisted it was too late.'

The adoption is something that saddens Pat to this day. 'I feel sorry that I did it, when I think of it. The pressure was on my parents as well. I think I would have got by ...' Wayne found out about Bradley when he was sixteen. He came across a letter from an adoption service organisation asking Pat to fill in a questionnaire, which would enable the agency to trace and locate Pat's son. Wayne asked his mum what the letter was about, and she sat him down and explained. Bradley contacted Pat when he was in his early twenties and was introduced to the family in Derby. He had only learned he had been adopted when he visited the graveyard where his brother was buried. He realised his brother's birth date was too close to his own.

This was still some years down the track. For the moment, life in Pat's house had settled into a calmer rhythm. She'd just met Ferdinand 'Ferdy' Bergmann, an Austrian-born Kimberley and Northern Territory bushman. For work, Ferdy constructed cattle yards, cattle dips, fences, water tanks and windmills. He drilled bores and could turn his hand to any manual task on a cattle station. He was respected and well liked by both Aboriginal and non-Aboriginal people. When Pat first met him, she had another bloke interested in her, a ringer, and there was a girl who was after Ferdy too, but these passions soon fizzled out.

According to Pat, 'Ferdy put himself right on my lap, and that was it!'

According to Ferdy, Pat needed to prove herself first.

When they were courting, Pat would visit Ferdy at his various job sites out bush. On one trip, Ferdy asked Pat to prepare them some lunch. There wasn't a frying pan. 'You'll have to cook the meat on the coals,' he told her. She cooked it beautifully, without a trace of grit, or dirt or charcoal. *I need to marry this girl*, Ferdy thought.

On another trip, Ferdy was building a new fence line near Mount Jowlaenga. He had strung a tarp over some poles and this gave him shade under which to work during the day. Pat visited one evening with Wayne in tow. Wayne woke in the middle of the night, busting to go for a poo. He didn't want to go in the bushes. He was scared of the dark, of the shadows of boabs. His Aunty Lena had told him about how, in the killing times, Aboriginal people were murdered and hung from their branches. He was frightened, too, of the min min lights. He knew if you saw the lights and followed their eerie glow into the bush, you might be grabbed, might never come back. With a pounding heart, Wayne crept out of his swag and pooed in the corner of Ferdy's work tent.

The next morning, Pat and Wayne took off before daybreak.

As the sky lightened, Ferdy was greeted with ribbons of dirty toilet paper.

It wasn't enough to deter him, and when the couple married, Pat asked Wayne if he would change his last name to Bergmann. With the change Wayne felt a subtle shift in his identity. Now he was no longer wholly defined by his Aboriginality but defined too by Ferdy's connections, particularly with people in the east and south Kimberley.

The family moved ten kilometres out of town to the old chook farm off the Gibb River Road on a block of sandy soil and bloodwoods. The bore spat salt, and fresh water had to be carted from town in 44 gallon drums. The only power was from an old single-cylinder Lister diesel generator, and this was used frugally for an hour or two in the evenings. Even so, Wayne's ears would ring long after it had been turned off. 'When you went to bed, you would think the generator's motor was still thumping.' There was no air-conditioning, no insulation, and initially the living space was limited to a concrete car garage fit for a single car. Ferdy converted the garage into a home, extending the roof and building wide wooden verandahs. He also kept a few pigs, and the children would play in the gum tree above their pen—though not without anxiety. Wayne says, 'We were always worried we'd fall in and the pigs would eat us!'

Wayne was also worried about disappointing his dad. He recalls they used a pump to water the mango saplings lining the block's perimeter. It was Wayne's job to cover the pump's motor to protect it from rain. But one time, he forgot. 'Dad kicked me in the guts. It was fucking brutal, that kick. Dad was extremely fit—he was ripped. *Don't you ever forget to cover up the motor again,* he said to me. I never did.'

One of the Bergmann's neighbours was Carol Martin, a woman who would go on to become the first Aboriginal woman elected to any parliament in Australia. Ferdy spent a lot of time with Carol's pop, and she recalls the two men were close, like mad professors when it came to inventions and ideas. They helped each other build sheds, distilled their own white-lightning schnapps and brooded on how to extract gas from pig poo.

Ferdy was also a gifted bush mechanic. Pat remembers lending him and a mate her car, an old brown station wagon, to go and hunt down a bullock for Christmas dinner. Wayne climbed into the back and the three set off up the Gibb River Road. They finally spotted a good bullock and chased it down across rough country, perforating the car's radiator on a stick along the way. This wasn't a problem for Ferdy. He opened the cow's guts and used the sticky grass inside to plug up the crack.

What was a problem was the police turning up a day later, on Christmas morning.

Someone had spied Ferdy dumping the leftover bullock at the edge of the marsh for the community dogs. They'd taken down Pat's numberplate.

The police bundled Ferdy into the paddy wagon. They'd already picked up his mate, and on the way to the station, the two men got their story straight. 'A cow ran onto the road. We hit it. And we thought, well, we can't just leave it there! We probably should cut it up and put it in the car!' The police couldn't work out the brand on the discarded skin—couldn't work out who the bullock belonged to. So they contacted one of the caretakers of a station along the Gibb River Road. The caretaker was an old bushie and a friend of Ferdy's. 'Poor blokes!' he said to the police. 'How's their car? Glad to hear they didn't waste the meat …'

Ferdy and his friend were free to return home for Christmas, but for a long time afterwards Ferdy would say, 'Watch out, Wayne. The police might come back, looking for a little blond-headed boy …'

It wasn't the first brush Ferdy had with the law. Once the police drove out to where he was camped on Mongrel Downs Station in the Northern Territory. They were delivering Ferdy a fine, likely for fighting. Upon seeing a growing plume of dust in the distance, Ferdy told his offsider to slice up some dingo for lunch and then to hide it. When they pulled up at the camp, Ferdy said, 'I've just put the billy on. Did you want a cuppa?'

'Sure, thanks,' the police said.

'How about some lunch? We're just about to have a feed.'

The police looked at each other. It was a long drive back to Alice Springs.

'Yeah, alright. Some lunch would be nice.'

Ferdy called to his offsider. 'Pull out that meat, will you?'

His offsider dragged the half-butchered dingo into view. There was still a paw hanging off it.

The police changed their minds about lunch.

Another time, in Fitzroy Crossing, Ferdy's drinking mate had been seized at the pub, the Crossing Inn, and thrown into jail for the night. Ferdy, irritated at losing his drinking partner, went and found a horse and some rope. He fastened the rope to the wall of the jail and ripped it down. Then the two men returned to the pub and kept drinking. This time when the police arrived they were both arrested. In the morning, the magistrate let Ferdy off with a warning: *Don't break any friends out of jail again.*

* * *

Wayne's Year 6 teacher, Tony Treacy, carries a photo around with him on his phone. It's of thirty Aboriginal schoolchildren with bright eyes and cheeky grins. The girls wear turquoise sack cloths, the boys are in prison grey. In front of their bare feet a placard reads: Holy Rosary Primary School Derby, 1979, Hostel. The children sit in four neat rows and are framed by a mango tree with glossy dark leaves and a rambling eucalypt with a bleached throat. Treacy's finger moves over their faces. 'Murder, suicide, accident …'

Six of the children are now dead.

Treacy couldn't imagine how profoundly his life would change when he moved to the Kimberley. He grew up outside of Goulburn and Tamworth in NSW, did his teacher training in Canberra, and knew the city wasn't for him. There was 'too much bush in the boy'. He was inspired to travel north after reading *Outlaws of the Leopolds*, a book from his grandfather's library. The book was about Jandamarra—the black Ned Kelly—a feared and intelligent Bunuba man who led a fierce guerrilla campaign against the white settlers. Bunuba country neighbours Nyikina country, and it was on Nyikina country that Treacy got his first job, as a volunteer at St Joseph's Hostel in Derby. The hostel provided accommodation for children from surrounding communities who were attending either Holy Rosary or the public school.

Living in Derby took some getting used to. There was no air-conditioning in the classes. When he leaned against the blackboard he left a shadow of sweat; when he marked homework, the pages stuck to his arm; and when he took the students on school camping trips, all hell broke loose. On one trip, out past the May River, the mosquitoes were so savage that in the middle of the night the children wriggled from their swags and jumped in the river to escape them.

Treacy taught Wayne in 1982, three years after the photo was taken. He remembers Wayne as a well-mannered and even-tempered young man. Wayne wasn't a sports star but held his own. He struggled with spelling but had the fundamentals. Treacy also recalls the family: Wayne's mum, Pat, was always respectful, and Nana Aggie was a matriarch of the church. 'Aggie would take over at funerals. People were not always sure of the protocols in the church and she'd make sure everyone was comfortable, she'd take on the role of usher, she'd let everyone know what was going on, and made sure the Father knew what was going on too. Aggie never seemed to age ...'

From a school perspective, Wayne came from a stable family.

From Wayne's perspective, school was difficult, especially reading and writing, and he would have preferred to be fishing with Aggie or his Uncle Cyril. One teacher made a huge impression on him at Holy Rosary: the stoic black South African Samuel Blommitjie. Blommitjie was in his sixties and had fled the Apartheid. He always dressed formally, in long pants, a tie and a jacket, even when the mercury surged above forty. He was also strict. One lunchtime Wayne wagged school with a friend. The two boys tore around the marsh on Wayne's motorbike, picked wild watermelons and didn't go back to school that day. When Blommitjie learned the boys had wagged, he took out his strap and called them to the front of the classroom. Wayne's friend was first. He tried to climb up the blackboard to avoid the burn of leather on the backs of his knees. 'Bergmann, you're next. *Don't you ever lie to me again …*'

Wayne's not sure if he screamed.

As the year progressed, Wayne continued to struggle. He felt acute shame in spelling tests, especially when he only got one or two words right out of fifteen. He started to cheat, scrawling the words on his hand or on bits of paper. This continued until Blommitjie shared with the class a perspective on life in South Africa.

'It's a place where people live in absolute poverty, where people have nothing, where people are getting robbed all the time. But they can't rob your knowledge. Your knowledge is the most important, the most powerful, thing you own.'

Wayne stopped cheating after that.

When he wasn't at school, Wayne would accompany his grandparents down to the reserve where people played cards and gambled in the shade. Nana Aggie sold dishes of curry and rice and Wayne sold mangoes, first for twenty cents each, then for fifty cents, then for a dollar. If mangoes were in short supply Wayne picked taylor fruit. The small income meant he could buy a pie or an ice-cream from the school tuckshop. This early business initiative revealed the blossoming of what would become a lifelong entrepreneurial spirit.

* * *

At age twelve Wayne went to boarding school in Perth. Trinity College was a Catholic school in the Edmund Rice tradition. Wayne liked the regular routine and enjoyed the luxury of three meals a day. In the city he was awed by the escalators in the shopping centres, though sometimes security guards tailed him through the shops—his first conscious experience of racism.

During one of his first weeks of high school, Wayne's science teacher asked him to find a test tube in the storeroom. Each piece of equipment was clearly labelled. But what *was* a test tube? What did a test tube even look like? He scanned the neatly packed shelves. Wayne identified the letter 't'. He made the sound nervously, tongue against palate. 'T … t … t …'

'Bergmann!' his teacher roared. 'What's taking you so long? What are you doing in there?'

He still couldn't read.

By this stage, the high school teachers were unable to help—they weren't trained in teaching basic literacy. So Trinity College offered assistance through the primary school. But Wayne was embarrassed. He didn't want his classmates to see him going for help at the primary school.

While Wayne had friends and got on well with his classmates, he was becoming more conscious of racism. One day a white student sneered at him, 'Boong, boong, boong.' Wayne weighed an orange in his hand, hard and tasteless, and then pegged it at the boy so viciously it splattered. 'The kid accepted his punishment. He knew he was guilty,' Wayne says.

In Year 9 a welcome diversion from study came in the form of Rugby Union. Wayne was selected for the school team. The first game of the season was against Wesley College. One of Wesley's players looked like he was eighteen—he had the dusky beginnings of a beard. Wayne was playing fullback and had just received a pass when the giant lined him up for a tackle. Wayne remembers the crack of the giant's knee against his collarbone, remembers hearing the bone snap. It was a miserable start to a school sporting career, but the following year things on the field would improve.

***

Pat noticed that when her children returned home to Derby during the school holidays, their attitude toward living in a small town had changed—there was confidence in the way they held themselves, an understanding of the wider world beyond the Kimberley. Pat was proud of her children, and she believed that it was up to them to work hard and to better themselves. She was also busy. Together with Ferdy she had three more children: Ferdinand Jnr, Martina and Cassandra. Counting his half-brothers and sisters, Wayne was one of eleven from his mother and biological father. This was sometimes problematic. One day he came out of the Derby Woolworths bewitched by the gorgeous girl on the checkout. 'Oh no,' his mum said. 'I gotta tell you something. That girl's your sister!'

That is when Wayne learned, at age sixteen, that he had a different father to his older sisters. He remembers wondering why his biological father didn't want anything to do with him.

School holidays weren't always spent in Derby. When Wayne got off the plane and saw Ferdy's truck all packed up with gear, a feeling of dread would slow his footsteps. A packed truck meant Ferdy was off to a job and Wayne would have to accompany him. 'I was fourteen, or fifteen, and I just wanted to go home, I wanted to mix and socialise. But Ferdy needed an offsider, and most blokes couldn't handle working with him. It would be stinking hot, you'd work all day, cook your own meals, and Dad's idea of "comfort" was almost unbearable for anyone else.'

On one trip, when Ferdy was working on Brooking Springs Station, he told Wayne that horse balls tasted pretty good. So Wayne went down to the yard where some old Bunuba men were drafting wild horses and cutting the balls off stallions to make geldings.

'I asked them for some horse balls and they looked at me, like, *This kid's mad! What does he want horse balls for?* The men had a fire going. They knocked over a little stallion and threw me the balls. I cooked them on the coals and ate them. Then I went back to Dad and said, *Yeah, horse balls do taste pretty good!* Dad burst out laughing and said, *I've never tried them.* Years later, when I was working in Fitzroy Crossing, those old Bunuba men remembered. *Ay! You're the kid who was eating horse balls at Brooking Springs!*'

During one school holiday Ferdy told Wayne they were heading to work on Quanbun Station and to pack the tuckerbox. Wayne packed enough food for the day. He had no idea he was in for a week-long trip. When they ran out of food, Wayne offered to drive to Fitzroy Crossing to stock up, but Ferdy wouldn't hear of it. That would be a waste of fuel and time.

'Here's a gun,' Ferdy told him. 'Go and shoot something.'

Wayne became good at identifying native foods: he shot pigeons, gathered bush oranges and collected sugarbag (wild honey) to sweeten Ferdy's tea. Wayne's younger brother, Ferdinand Jnr, was also roped in to work trips, and he would climb up windmills to steal crows' eggs for breakfast. Wayne learned to plan, and to plan for the worst, as often he would have to look after himself or go hungry.

Wayne remembers Ferdy didn't eat much. 'Dad was lean, he could live off the smell of an oily rag. Sometimes, when we went out with him, he wouldn't think to bring anything for us kids. One time, when I was only seven or eight, I went camping for the night with Dad and a group of mates. As the afternoon went on, I got thirsty and asked Dad for a drink of water. But he hadn't packed any water, all they had was beer. *Drink this,* Dad said. It was disgusting, I couldn't handle the taste, I spat it out.'

When Ferdy wasn't working hard, he was playing hard—usually in the long break over the wet season. He'd stock up on a pallet of Emu Export cartons and invite his mates around. As the afternoons lengthened and the men lost the buzz of beer, they switched to overproof rum. One morning Ferdy asked one of his drinking mates to help him lift a bit of wood. The man had been on the piss hard for four months straight. Before the first few drinks of the day, he'd have the shakes. The piece of wood had a nail jutting from its side. It slipped from the man's fingers and the nail landed on his foot, drove all the way to the bone. Wayne recalls looking at the place the nail had punctured and seeing a single trembling marble of fluid. It was congealed; it was as if the man bled pure alcohol.

Then, when all the beer and rum were gone, Ferdy would head back out bush. He would stay off the piss and work his guts out.

* * *

By Year 10, Wayne was an asset to the school rugby team. He'd been moved to inside centre, on account of his speed, and was playing for his school, for Cottesloe and for his state. He remembers travelling to Queensland to compete in the Australian Championships with WA's state team, and then coming back to Perth and feeling really low, a post-adrenaline dip. He was also increasingly self-conscious of his inability to read or write. The basketball coach doubled as an English teacher, and after training one day Wayne asked if the coach could help him with his literacy. The coach said, 'Don't worry about it. Just finish the basketball season.'

The coach's response dispirited Wayne so much that he quit school, moved back to Derby and got into some serious trouble.

Trouble came in the form of two young men. The first had

his own car, a V8. The second was a former foster child who had suffered horrific abuse and had just been released from prison. One night the boys piled into the car and went for a cruise. They parked at the edge of the marsh. A low tide had exposed the spidery legs of the mangroves. They fired up a joint and became deliriously high then dangerously hungry. The owner of the car stayed behind and Wayne and his other mate headed off to find food.

Ice-cream. They needed ice-cream.

Wayne's mate suggested breaking into the school. There were boxes of ice-cream in the school's canteen. No-one would know. What they hadn't accounted for was the alarm system: the siren was ear-splitting. They quickly ran away.

The next stop on their spree was the local pool. With some difficulty, they levered open the pool gate, smashed a window made from thick glass and beelined for the freezers. Then, with the sizzle of ice-cream sugar in their blood, they stole some scuba diving tanks and decided to head home. On the way they broke into the chemist with a screwdriver and stole a pile of comics.

It was the early hours of the morning by the time Wayne snuck into Nana Aggie's house. He was awoken midmorning by a thumping on his bedroom door.

'Wayne!' Aggie shouted. 'This policeman wants to talk to you! What did you do?'

'I didn't do anything,' Wayne said. 'I don't know what you're talking about.'

'You hear him?' Aggie challenged the policeman. 'He said he didn't do anything! He said he doesn't know what you're talking about!'

Wayne was hauled to the police station. He kept up the fiction, claiming innocence, until he saw his mum. That's when he was overcome. He broke down into tears and confessed. The police knew he was responsible for the break and enters—the other boy had dobbed him in.

Carol Martin, the Bergmann's neighbour, was assigned as Wayne's welfare officer. She wasn't worried about him, knew he was a courteous child from a good family. 'It's not hard to be nice to a good kid, and one little spree with a mob of peers doesn't make a criminal. As a first offender, Wayne wasn't charged. There was no conviction recorded. The kids had nothing else to do. They were bored. It was a bit of an adrenaline hit …'

After the incident, Wayne went before the court. Carol recalls, 'Wayne was very quiet, very well presented, very ashamed. The magistrate gave Wayne a roasting. He was of the opinion that if he didn't pull Wayne up now, Wayne might end up in places he didn't want to be.' Carol says there was an additional shame for the teenager, too, the burning shame of having let down his family. 'People had placed great expectations on him, whether he knew it or not at the time.'

Wayne did know it at the time.

Not long after, still desperately ashamed, he got a hold of his grandpa's .22 gun and contemplated suicide. He might have become another statistic. He might have become like one of the dead children in Tony Treacy's photo—if he'd found the bullets.

Pat was philosophical about Wayne's night-time misadventure. 'We just took everything as it came.'

Carol told the family that Wayne should be sent back to school. 'Ferdy was really hard on Wayne. He was hard as rocks. Wayne needed an education; he didn't need to work for his dad.'

But Ferdy, considering Wayne's consistently poor marks,

couldn't see the point. For the next eight months, Wayne worked with Ferdy, drilling bores, building windmills and fencing. One of the jobs was on Quanbun Station, and it was during this job Wayne fell in love for the first time. The girl was a freckled, red-haired Texan studying animal husbandry. She was older than him, twenty-three to his sixteen, and from a wealthy family. Wayne would sneak out at night to meet the girl down by the river and then return to camp before sun-up to light the fire and boil the billy ready for Ferdy's morning cuppa. One evening he did the long walk to Birdwood Downs only to find that the girl had disappeared. Her dad had died and she'd flown home to Texas.

Wayne was heartbroken.

* * *

Although he'd never finished school, Wayne's Catholic education and upbringing had instilled in him a sense of justice and fairness, a template for judging right and wrong. He'd also acquired Ferdy's sterling work ethic, and it wasn't long before he secured a metal fabrication apprenticeship in Perth. He was a confident young man but recalls a sense of shame when he started. 'I had no money, no nothing. So, I went off to the second-hand store and got a pair of overalls and some old boots. After three months, Australian Shipbuilding Industries sorted me out with a uniform …'

It was 1986, the year Wayne turned seventeen, and he was living in Rockingham, south of Perth, with his older sister Helen and her boyfriend, who was a police officer. The job was a breeze after working for Ferdy, and he was taken under the wing of an old skilled tradesman from South America. In his first year Wayne learned to cut metal for prawn trawlers and tuna boats. A year later he was promoted to the more technical work of building South Pacific patrol vessels for the navy.

At TAFE Wayne's lecturers commented on his 'excellent start to training' and complimented his positive progress and attitude. He was awarded almost straight A's for each year of his apprenticeship. In his spare time Wayne trained with the army reserve and competed as an amateur boxer. On completion of his apprenticeship he received a glowing reference from one of his supervisors. M. Patience wrote, 'He has been a willing and conscientious worker and I would have no hesitation in recommending him for employment elsewhere.'

'Elsewhere', for the time being, was back in the Kimberley with his dad. Wayne clocked up long hours on the boat with Ferdy—who by then had a professional barramundi fishing licence—and this allowed him to attain his coxswain certificate. 'I knew there was no way in hell I was gunna become a professional fisherman. I had images of crocs jumping at me and my hands were cut up by fish spines and cracked by the cold.' The pair slept in swags on the boat's deck and it was anything but serene—a generator ran twenty-four seven to power the onboard freezers.

Ferdy had other staff working on the boat and under contract to do jobs. Wayne learned the finer points of bookkeeping from his Uncle Cyril, and was soon paying wages, deducting tax and chasing invoices. He was also alert to opportunities that might help his dad. Back during the first year of his apprenticeship, he had brokered a deal with Kailis Fish Market. 'Dad and I are here and we're gunna make a name for ourselves,' he told one of Kailis's sales executives. 'We'd like to set up a supply chain with barramundi fillets. If you can send us the boxes, we'll send you the fillets.' Kailis agreed to the deal and sent four big carts of boxes to Derby. 'But Dad never sold them a single fillet. He sold his barra to everyone else. We eventually had to pay them back for the boxes …'

Tension between father and son was heightening and soon the two men had 'the biggest blue'. Wayne recalls Ferdy owed him two thousand dollars after he'd finished jobs on Quanbun and Jubilee stations. 'But Dad refused to pay me. We didn't speak to each other for two or three years. I haven't worked for him since.'

After that, Wayne picked up his own contract to build a holding paddock for cattle on Quanbun with his friend Alan 'Doodie' Lawford. It was April, at the very tail of the wet season, and the soil was so boggy the men couldn't get to the site to do the job. By this time Wayne urgently needed money. He applied for several boilermaker/welder positions and while waiting to hear back, Doodie suggested he consider going for the trainee art coordinator position at Mangkaja Arts in Fitzroy Crossing.[7] Wayne thought about it. What did he have to lose?

It was a pivotal moment: the opening at Mangkaja would set the entire course of his adult life, and his friendship with Doodie would, many years later, result in the establishment of the largest one-hundred-percent Aboriginal-owned cattle venture in northern Australia.

3: If you can make it in Fitzroy, you can make it anywhere

Fitzroy Crossing was two and a half hours by road from Derby, further up the Martuwarra, on Bunuba country. Here, the river was bordered with eucalypts, hummock grasslands and scattered vine thickets. Sometimes, in a big wet, the single-lane highway sank beneath floodways of muddy water. On the morning Wayne drove into town for his job interview, the highway was clear but for the occasional skittish cow.

Wayne pulled up outside Karrayili Adult Education Centre, of which Mangkaja Arts was then a part. Karrayili operated from an old building where exposed electrical cords sparked and smoked, fans fell from the ceiling in shivers of plaster, and visitors staying overnight were kept awake by the rhythmic chewing of termites. For the most part, the staff were able to shrug off the building's quirks and keep focused. But two of the staff lost focus, just for a moment, when Wayne appeared outside their office window. At twenty-two years old, Christine Keeffe was Karrayili's principal; she'd trained as a teacher and had grown up on a wheat and sheep farm in Mullewa, in the state's Mid West.

Her friend and colleague nudged her. 'Who's that bloke? He's pretty cute …'

Chris followed her friend's gaze. The young man was of medium stature, fit from station work, with intense hazel eyes and olive skin. Later, when he smiled, she would notice a becoming gap between his two front teeth. 'Yeah,' she agreed. 'He looks alright!'

Wayne didn't realise he was under scrutiny; he was too busy thinking about the interview and Karrayili. The centre had been established by a group of Walmajarri people in the 1980s to teach adults English. The group wanted their mob to be able to communicate with kartiyas, represent themselves to government, and to be able to sign cheques with their names, instead of X's. As it was, they felt they were being 'left on the side of the road' (McGinty 7). Joyce Hudson, a linguist and former staff member, was once approached by an old lady asking for help to change her name by deed poll. Many of the old people who grew up on the stations were given names by the white bosses. This old lady's name was Peanut. Perhaps it had once been an endearing name but the lady was no longer a child, and she'd just found out what the word 'peanut' meant.

Initially led by local men, Karrayili's activities also involved visual art. As part of literacy classes, students painted stories, bush trips and histories. Artists would sell their work directly to tourists from a windowless property of concrete and tin, built in the shape of a fifty-cent coin. Later, unscrupulous art dealers would swoop in, provide people with canvases, pay them a pittance, then sell their work for top dollar at galleries around Australia.

In 1988 the distinct bough-shed series of gift cards (arising from a collaboration with Magabala Books) was published, launching the careers of some of Fitzroy's finest artists. When Karen Dayman arrived in town in 1990 with a background in gallery administration, she was excited by both the established and emerging art scenes. She worked with the economic development project officer at Karrayili to secure funding to train a young Aboriginal art coordinator.

Wayne was interviewed for the job by Karen and some of Karrayili's founding members at the Mangkaja Arts shopfront, a short distance from Karrayili. The questions were straightforward.

'They asked, *Do you drink*? I said nup. *Do you smoke*? Nup. *Have you got a wife*? Nup.'

He was hired, on a base salary of eighteen thousand dollars a year.

For the first week he stayed with an aunty. He was grateful for her hospitality and generosity, but quickly became wearied and worried by the twenty-four-hour traffic of people coming, going and drinking. He was upfront with Karen. 'I think I'm going to have to quit unless I can get some decent accommodation …' The housing shortage in Fitzroy Crossing meant finding any accommodation was difficult. Karen came up with a solution. Karrayili's principal, Chris, lived alone in a three-bedroom house. She was heading to East Timor for Easter and agreed to rent Wayne a room while she was away. He'd have to move out when she got back—Chris liked her space.

Wayne was glad for a quiet, albeit temporary, place to live, and glad to be in Fitzroy. 'In those days, raw culture was still being practised. People would walk past the art centre in tracksuits soaked with blood. They'd been speared for tribal punishment. No-one blinked an eye. There were strong cultural rules and people behaved. I also met many men and women who had nothing, who would die with nothing. But they stood up for what was right and they were warriors, with an ability to lead at the front and command respect and authority without question.'

Wayne liked his job at Mangkaja. The space was both an art gallery and a workshop, open during the day for people to paint in. Many of the old people Wayne worked with could remember walking in off the desert and seeing white people for the first time. The artists brought to their work a profound knowledge of country, and sometimes profound sadness.

While she was painting, Daisy Andrews reflected on all the old people who had suffered harm at the hands of police and station owners. One of her paintings depicts the place her father was shot dead by trackers. As she worked on this piece, she thought of blood. When Walmajarri man Pompey 'Jitirn' Siddon painted, he remembered his father being hauled back to a cattle station in chains. On one occasion, the police beat his father so badly he couldn't walk, couldn't carry the chains.

There was a social justice aspect to Mangkaja's work, too. Wayne coordinated the development of a mural in Fitzroy prison that depicted a vicious cycle: no money, get drunk, have a fight, go to jail. The mural was vivid and colourful, offering gentle encouragement to inmates not to make the same mistakes again. He also ran a project with Pompey. The two would pick up a group of young prisoners from the jail, and then they'd take them out on country and teach them to make boomerangs.

Karen was grateful to have a hard worker on board and she recognised Wayne was ambitious. She knew he felt a deep sense of responsibility as a young Aboriginal person, a sense that at some point he would need to step up into a more significant position. 'Wayne said, quite clearly, that he found the responsibility daunting. He wasn't sure if he was ready for it ...'

Maree Gaffney, also a former Karrayili staff member, remembers Wayne as a thoughtful young man during his Fitzroy years. 'He was quite self-contained, possibly shy and he was a bit of an observer. He never spoke before considering what he said. When he said something, you knew it wouldn't be flippant.'

Not long after starting, Wayne received a lucrative job offer in the oil and gas industry. The job was with United Construction and it involved building an oil and gas platform off the Burrup Peninsula, an area famed for its concentration of exquisite rock art. Wayne would be on a base salary of fifty thousand dollars a year plus penalty rates—significantly more than what he was earning at the arts centre. He was tempted, and not just by the money. Karrayili's principal, Chris, was due back from East Timor in a matter of days. When she got back, Wayne would have nowhere to live.

* * *

Two years earlier, Chris had arrived in the Kimberley from WA's Mid West, armed with a pocketknife from her worried dad. She had a job working as a primary school teacher at Gogo School, and a dream to save up enough money to travel the world. She thought Fitzroy Crossing would be a sleepy backwater, a place with nowhere to go and nothing to do but save for the trip.

Instead, she encountered a dynamic community where Walmajarri, Bunuba, Wangkatjungka and Gooniyandi people lived and worked side by side. It wasn't long before she became captivated: exhilarated by the people, the lifestyle and her work.

'From my perspective as a white person, I didn't see the segregation. I saw Aboriginal people mixing with white people. This was completely different to where I'd grown up. I had the impression that everyone got on and I was oblivious to the racism … This was during the years of ATSIC and there was a really good feeling in town.[8] There was a feeling of people taking control, setting up outstations and moving back to country. It was an empowering time, a great place to be, an amazing political space.'

On weekends Chris went fishing for barramundi, caught cherrabun (freshwater shrimp), explored ancient cave systems, and backstroked across waterholes. She had a great sense of humour and a natural rapport with the children at school. Having grown up on a farm, she was also wary of snakes.

During Chris's first year at Gogo, a couple of staff from the Perth Museum came to visit and they stayed with Chris and her housemate. The visitors were obsessed with snakes—especially Children's pythons—and upon catching one they asked Chris if she would like a hold. Chris said she would. With the reptile placidly draped over her arm, her mind began to whir. What if she caught a python and brought it into her pre-primary class? Imagine the language experience it would generate! Each week, the children focused on a letter of the alphabet. Serendipitously, this week's letter was 's'.

The next day, on her way to school, Chris saw a half-dead snake stretched out on the road. It looked like it had been clipped by a car tyre. It looked like a python. Perfect! She emptied her woven African handbag, found a long stick, and gently lifted the snake into the bag. Then she tied it up and placed it next to her on the front seat of the panel van. When she got to school, she thought she had better check that it actually was a python, before showing it to her class. The gardener and some children crowded around as she opened her handbag over an empty aquarium. The snake tumbled out—heavy, ropy, deadly. The students screamed and bolted for the windows and doors. It wasn't a python at all but a venomous king brown.

After two years at Gogo School, Chris received an unexpected offer. The principal of Karrayili Adult Education Centre was leaving, and he encouraged Chris to apply for his job. It seemed like a long shot—she had no expertise and had only been a teacher for a couple of years. But she put in an application and was successful in securing an interview.

The interview was a clinic in brevity and Traditional Owner priorities.

'The old people asked, *Can you mow the lawn?* I said yep. *Can you use a chainsaw?* I said yep. *If we go hunting, can you sit with us, and wait patiently, all day, and not be one of those kartiya who packs up too quickly?* I said yep.'

Chris got the job and put her dreams of drifting the world on hold. Instead, she made the most of her annual leave—this year it was East Timor—and she came home feeling refreshed. But upon arrival at the house she was nettled to find the trainee arts coordinator still living in one of her rooms.

* * *

Wayne was torn whether to take the oil and gas job or not. He discussed the decision with some friends at the Crossing Inn. The Crossing Inn was one of two pubs in town. There was a lounge bar inside chilled with air-conditioning, an 'animal bar' out the back with concrete walls and a metal grid through which drinks were served, and a garden bar strung with warm lights and hemmed in by boabs and gums. By the time Wayne had moved to Fitzroy Crossing, the pub was part Aboriginal-owned. In 1987, the community had formed an investment company to buy shares in several businesses in town, including the Crossing Inn. The decision to buy the pub was controversial. Drinking was a problem in Fitzroy. From light aircraft, visitors and passengers observed 'Fitzroy snow'—silver lakes of beer cans discarded around popular drinking spots. But community members, like Bunuba man Patrick Green, figured if local Aboriginal people didn't buy the pub, someone else would. Here was an opportunity to generate income, to be less reliant on government, and to manage the problem themselves.

In Patrick's view, Fitzroy Crossing was, and remains, a strong traditional town and a political hotspot. 'Aboriginal people very much run the town. The town was built around us. We can either make things happen, or we don't.' It was clear to Patrick that Wayne was the kind of person who could make things happen. 'He was always a confident young fella and a go-getter. Knowing his dad, Wayne had no choice but to learn.'

The two friends caught up over a game of pool in the lounge bar at the Crossing Inn. Before long they were joined by another Bunuba man, Dickie Bedford, and also by Nyikina man Robert Watson. The young men passed around the cue, lined up the balls, and cleared inches off their beers. 'So ...' Wayne said, 'I think I'm off to the Pilbara, to build an offshore oil and gas platform.'

There were back slaps, grins and the clinking of cold pint glasses. Then Patrick rubbed his chin and fell silent.

'What?' Wayne asked.

'Well, it's just ... why would you leave? If you can make it in Fitzroy Crossing, you can make it anywhere in the world.'

It was Wayne's turn to fall into a thoughtful silence. Work at Mangkaja, while poorly paid, was challenging and fulfilling. And though he wasn't quite ready to admit it, he was starting to fall in love with his housemate, Chris. A few nights previous, when he knew she was working late, he thought he'd impress her by cooking dinner—a real gourmet meal. He rinsed two cups of white rice and carefully measured out the water before putting it on to boil. He heated two tablespoons of vegetable oil and browned wedges of onion. And then he warmed up the 'tin dog', the canned beef. The meal was completed with a lick of tomato sauce. When Chris arrived home from work, she took one look and mumbled an apology. 'Sorry, I've already had dinner, thank you.'

Chris wasn't interested in Wayne. Not yet, anyway. But when he'd told her about the job offer, she began to feel guilty.

'I knew if Wayne moved out and took the job, then Mangkaja would lose him. Karen had been looking for someone for ages, and Wayne was doing a really good job there, stretching canvases, making display boxes, helping the old people. So, I felt pressured. And he wasn't an untidy boarder. He was handy with a broom and he wasn't afraid to scrub the toilet …'

Chris relented and told Wayne he was welcome to keep renting. It was this offer, along with Patrick's words at the pub that night, that made up his mind.

* * *

A few months later, the housemates found themselves working together on a major project. Tandanya National Aboriginal Cultural Institute Inc. was eager to host an exhibition of artwork by the Karrayili artists. The artists wanted to travel to Adelaide for the opening night. An important Traditional Owner called 'Double A', Adam Andrews, had an old orange school bus. It didn't go over eighty kilometres an hour, there was no bullbar, no tow ball, and the floor of the bus was like a colander. But it had recently been fitted with a new motor, and Double A was confident it could make the trip. Wayne and Chris worked together to fix up the bus and when it came time to head off, they sat up the front—they were the only two with licences to drive a bus. As they drove, dust billowed through the cracks in the floor. Chris remembers, 'At one of the stops, when we climbed out covered in red from head to toe, people thought we were on the way to law business.'

Somewhere along the Duncan Road the axle on the trailer gave way and the bus slowed to a halt. The Karrayili students from Bayulu wrote, 'Being a Derby boy, Wayne was a bit of a bushman and knew how to deal with emergencies like this. He clipped a bit of fencing wire from a nearby fence and wrapped it around the axle to hold the trailer together. He did a good job. The trailer lasted until we got to Alice Springs where we got it fixed' (McGinty 35).

It was an eventful trip—a frillneck lizard was barbecued for dinner, an old lady lost her swag to thieves, and one night Wayne shot a giant kangaroo. Everyone seemed pleased and tucked into it with relish. But the next morning some of the old people became anxious. Chris recalls them murmuring, 'That kangaroo too big ... We think you shot the Dreamtime kangaroo ...'

The exhibition ran from 15 September to 3 November 1991. The Bayulu Karrayili artists described their trip to Adelaide this way: 'We finally saw our paintings hanging in a gallery and understood what an exhibition was. Then we turned around and spent another eight days in Adam's bus to get back to Fitzroy Crossing' (McGinty 35).

On the drive home, Chris began to really warm to Wayne. 'I'd grown up around people who were good with their hands but among the blokes there were a lot of chauvinists. Wayne was good with his hands and he could fix anything, but he wasn't chauvinistic or sexist. Something that stood out for me on that Tandanya trip was that he was so kind to the old people, he treated them with such respect.'

One old lady decided that Wayne and Chris would make a good couple. So she sung them. All the way to Adelaide and all the way home, she sang traditional love songs. In the years after the trip, the old people would say, 'You got together because we sung you!' or, 'It's not true love, you mob were sung!'

In any case, the magic worked, and by the time Wayne was ready to take the next challenging step in his career, Chris was right there by his side.

* * *

When Wayne started at the Kimberley Aboriginal Law and Culture Centre in 1993, there was a black-and-white photograph of his Nana Aggie in the office. Aggie was wearing a dress and was mid-stride in the front row of a group of protesters walking down a wide street in Broome. The protesters—Aboriginal women, children and men— carried handpainted signs with the words 'justice', 'fairly' and 'white man—manslaughter acquitted'. They marched against a backdrop of palm trees, gum trees and frangipanis. They marched in the aftermath of the savage killing of a young Aboriginal man in 1988.

Two non-Aboriginal men had been involved. Peter Wicks was twenty-three and unemployed. His friend, James Dyson, had a job and accommodation at the Continental Hotel in Broome. On 16 June, Wicks settled in with a beer at the Continental Hotel at around noon. Seven hours later, he stumbled onward to the Roebuck Bay Hotel—a pub originally built to cater for the hard-drinking crews off the pearl luggers—where he drained between thirty and thirty-five middies of beer (*Wicks* 3). After eleven o'clock that night he returned to the Continental Hotel to join Dyson for further drinks in his friend's room.

At some point he became aware of a young man sitting quietly in Dyson's car.

The backseat of the car had been doubling as Wicks's bed.

Who the fuck was cheeky enough to be sitting on his bed?

The two men lurched down to the car park to find out.

* * *

Leslie Sampi was twenty years old and son of the Kimberley Land Council's then-chairperson, Patrick Sampi. He had an intellectual disability and was virtually deaf. Wicks pulled Leslie from the car by the scruff of his neck, knocked him unconscious, dragged him thirty metres and then booted him so hard he tore the membrane which held Leslie's bowel together. Then he kicked Leslie's heart until it was torn from its walls. A piece of concrete caught his attention. He picked it up and used it to cave Leslie's head in.

When the judge asked what was on his mind, Wicks said, 'Still nothing, you know; as I said, like a machine or something. It's just blank' (*Wicks* 11).

Dyson warned Wicks that he might kill the young man and Wicks shook himself, dropped the concrete. But as he backed off, he noticed a knife on the backseat of Dyson's car.

He used it to slit Leslie's throat from ear to ear.

The all-white jury found Wicks guilty of manslaughter but not murder.

Dyson walked free.

The verdict prompted outrage among the Aboriginal community; it sparked a huge protest in Broome, of which Wayne's Nana Aggie was a part. Leslie's dad and Kimberley Land Council chair, Patrick Sampi, in a letter to the Derby newspaper *The Boab Battler*, wrote,

'The thing that upsets us is those two men went on the bench and said in court that they had killed my son. The evidence was there. It was shown in court—the knife and the brick. The witness agreed to go out and have a look at the body, which was lying face down. What else does the jury want to administer justice?'

A couple of paragraphs further on he continued, 'My traditional law is that the father must stay until the Spirit tells me I can go back to my family. My belief is that I can't go until justice is done. I have no peace in my mind or heart. What can I do? All I want is justice. I've got nothing left. I feel my son was not defended in Court. He was "thrown away" like a dead cat or dog' (Sampi).

It seemed evident nothing had changed in over a hundred years.

Back in 1889, the attorney-general of Western Australia wrote, 'I despair of ever seeing justice done to the natives. White men may shoot a poor black boy in a tree or roast off a man's private parts, and no jury will convict' (Marchant 41).

* * *

With Nana Aggie's photo watching over him, Wayne threw himself into learning about Aboriginal customary law. He'd been appointed as the new coordinator for KALACC—his position was equivalent to chief executive. He answered to the board and to his chair, senior Walmajarri law boss Joe Brown. Joe enjoyed working with Wayne. 'Wayne was just a young fella [when he started], but his heart was very big, and he talked very strong ... At meetings, Wayne never could talk at the front. I would talk first, and he would talk after.'

For Kimberley Aboriginal people, customary law wasn't just about punishment or the art of justice. Yawuru man and Labor Senator Pat Dodson described it as the basis of governance in

Aboriginal affairs. 'Customary Law is an all-encompassing reality. There are the secret-sacred aspects, men's business or women's business; then there's the broader protocol and reciprocity that applies under the kinship structures and systems; and then there's the protocols of behaviour in relation to people and country, and people outside of your own group, and the respect and recognition you provide to others for where they belong and how they conduct their affairs and business. There are many obligations and responsibilities and structures of accountability in customary Law' (La Fontaine 15).

Yawuru leader Peter Yu observed the way white law and customary law operated beside each other. Customary law, prior to the establishment of KALACC, had an expression limited to a cultural context, and was dominated by white law. Peter said the establishment of KALACC linked the political movement of Kimberley Aboriginal people to cultural authority.

For Joe Brown, law and culture meant the law of the ground. 'People were born and lived in this land and they treated it according to our Law. All the Law and stories we were taught by the old people. A person's own country is just like a mother. Important ground alright. That's why we need to teach everyone the Law for that ground' (La Fontaine 15).

Part of KALACC's mission was to promote the ceremonies, songs and dances of Kimberley Aboriginal people. Wayne was tasked with organising a festival, the Garinba Junba; it would be the first KALACC had run since 1984. 'I had no admin skills. No training. I sent a letter to a heap of mining companies and corporations asking them to donate money. No-one did.' Fortunately, Wayne secured a grant through the Australia Council for the Arts, and he used this to prepare the site at Dunham River Gorge on the

Aboriginal-owned Doon Doon Station. The festival was held in the school holidays so children could attend—it was important to build up the next generation. Wayne ordered pallets of watermelons and oranges, and organised a street hawker to cook hot food. He strung up hessian and dug pit toilets. He remembers copping abuse for not organising interpreters. 'I was so stressed. I'd been dry-retching all week during the festival. It wasn't as if I was some kind of cookie-cutter CEO! I was trying to work for everyone. I remember Ivan McPhee coming up to me and saying, *Hey, Bubagee. What can I do to help?* He was one of the cornerstones of my early growth.'

Ivan McPhee, a Nyikina and Walmajarri man who chaired the Kimberley Land Council between 1993 and 1998, had been checking in with Wayne regularly since he started the job. 'He used to ring me every three weeks, or six weeks, and ask how I was going. He'd call from his community and say, *Wayne, I'm just checking in. I haven't heard you on the radio!* Or he'd say, *I heard you on the radio, keep it up, Brother! I know everyone's running you down, don't you listen to them. I know you're doing a good job.* He had old values, was a great human being to be around, and was so attuned to right and wrong, and to justice. He was one of those mob who would encourage you to walk on water.'

Pulling the festival off was almost as challenging as walking on water. But when it was finally underway, Wayne found all the stress had been worth it—the energy was electric. Mobs from across the Kimberley performed public dances, and it became almost competitive, with each dance more powerful than the last, with each group proudly showing off their culture.

Joe Brown fondly recalls those early festivals. 'The East Kimberley and the West Kimberley would come together every night. There were people from Wyndham, the Gibb River, Paruku ... a big three-day festival. There were campfires everywhere and people were singing all night long. They were really happy times—everyone could meet up. We'd start early and it would take a long time to finish the festival. We had strong ladies too, and strong lady singers. These days, our old people have passed, and it's changed now. But in the early days, there was a lot of support.'

There was only one pitfall at that first junba, and it occurred when the Gibb River mob danced with certain symbols that caused upset among the desert mobs. The desert women ducked and screamed and covered their faces. The desert men walked away. The next day, all the old men held a meeting to discuss the issue. When it was resolved, they shook hands, and that was the end of it.

It was a big cultural lesson for Wayne.

'I watched the way the old people sorted out this issue. I learned you've got to be honest with yourself and with each other. That means saying things honestly, saying things people don't always want to hear. You need to be able to sort it out then and there. The problem doesn't leave the circle. Once you shake hands, you don't carry any bad feeling away with you. The issue has been resolved. That was the richness I remember.'

After the junba, Wayne said to Chris, 'I can't believe I get paid to do this job.' But Chris recognised that Wayne's poor literacy was still holding him back. 'His reading and writing was probably at a grade-one level. For the first festival he had signs made up with the words "Dunham River George" instead of "Dunham River Gorge". His literacy was that low.' Wayne kept an exercise book full of numerals, against which the numbers were spelled out in letters. This helped him write cheques.

Maree Gaffney, who recalled Wayne as self-contained and observant, was now firm friends with the couple. She taught Wayne the art of writing funding submissions. 'He was such a quick learner—thirsty for knowledge. He wanted to know how to do things independently, wanted to learn the space and be good at it, and he didn't want to have to rely on other people too much. I think Wayne was always quite driven and that has played out across his whole life.'

Chris is amazed that Wayne never had a hang-up about his poor literacy. 'Wayne doesn't get embarrassed. This is possibly because he was really good at sport at school and he had confidence from this. But that said, he's never hidden anything. He doesn't have an embarrassed bone in his body.'

Another of Wayne's early jobs at KALACC was arranging for the repatriation of several sacred objects that had appeared for auction through Sotheby's. He wrote to Robert Tickner—the minister for Aboriginal and Torres Strait Islander affairs in Bob Hawke's government—lobbying him for money to repatriate the 'secret *scared* objects'. Despite the misspelling, he was successful in securing funds. Joe Brown offered to travel to Perth to pick them up. The objects were powerful and the old people were worried that if they were flown back to country, the plane might crash.

'I said to Joe, *Look, I'm putting five thousand dollars cash in this bag for fuel and accommodation. All I need is for you to put the receipts in the bag and bring the receipts back.* So off Joe went with this big bag of money. And when he returned to Fitzroy a couple of weeks later with the secret sacred objects, every single receipt was in there, every dollar was accounted for.'

Joe Brown remembers the trip too. When he came home and people asked him about the money, he said, 'We already used it all, and we gotta be careful with what we're doing.' To Wayne he said, 'You treat me with respect, you get respect back.'

Joe Brown knew that respect and listening to the old people were fundamental to keeping culture strong. He was born on Noonkanbah Station and grew up mustering and droving. His brother taught him to break in horses. 'That time, we think of it as a hard time, but it was just interesting.'

Joe Brown always had a strong sense of his language and culture. After the KALACC years, during the Kimberley Land Council days, he was invited on a trip to Europe with Yawuru man Peter Yu and Nyikina man John Watson. He gave a talk to a huge crowd of indigenous peoples from around the world. 'I talked in my language. I told them: We still travel our country. My people bin come from the bush … my grandpa, grandmother, my dad, and my brother. I was born and became a river boy. A Fitzroy boy. We go hunting for turkey and emu. We go fishing. That's how we live …'

The crowd looked on, bewildered.

'These people didn't understand, me talking Walmajarri!'

Joe Brown was one of the driving forces behind the Yiriman Project, an initiative to build stories in young people, particularly young people at risk. It came about through seeing a couple of young fellas who wouldn't listen to anyone. Joe Brown talked about the problem with two other senior men, Nyikina brothers John and Harry Watson. They wondered, 'What are we gunna do about these terrible kids?' The men devised a plan to take the young people out on camels from Jarlmadangah community. They'd show them the river and would teach them to fish, to catch goannas, and to clean and cook kangaroos the proper way. Around the campfire in the evenings they'd tell them stories.

Maree Gaffney and John Watson worked on the initial funding application together. They were successful in locking in both funds and a coordinator, and on the very first trip the boys were away for a month. They came back changed: tight with each other and very connected to culture. Joe Brown later observed, 'Young people still want to learn culture, but they're going in that different way (Western). That's what's happening. They get confused. We're trying to bring them back, make them really strong … If they lose language and connection to culture they become a nobody inside and that's enough to put anyone over the edge' ('The Elders' Report' 9).

One of those first two boys, years later, approached Joe Brown down at the footy field and said, 'You mob bin take me to the desert.'

'He was really friendly, this boy,' Joe Brown recalls. 'I couldn't believe it. He became a really good footballer.'

That's how the Yiriman Project started.

'Yiriman was for Walmajarri, right down to Bidyadanga. It was about walking in two ways, the kartiya way, and to be taught by the old people. You go this way, you're going to be killed. You go this way, you're going to be saved.'

Joe Brown speaks from experience.

He lost a seventeen-year-old son and a sixteen-year-old granddaughter to suicide.

* * *

Against this backdrop of dramatic light and shade Wayne and Chris continued to forge a life together. They planned their wedding for 8 April 1995, but as the date neared, so did a cyclone—Tropical Cyclone Chloe was shaping up to be the most intense storm of the season. Ferdy was anxious about the road being cut off between Derby and Broome, so he didn't make it. Uncle Cyril couldn't attend either; he was stranded by floodwaters at Beagle Bay. The cyclone wasn't the only hurdle. Chris had originally dreamed of being married on the beach but the priest refused—it was the church or nothing. He was surprised the couple were still together and is rumoured to have said, 'I never thought they would have lasted … I thought Chris was marrying the cause.' There was also the vexing issue of the guest list. Wayne and Chris had arranged for a bus to travel to Broome from Fitzroy Crossing to transport the old people from Mangkaja and Karrayili. The bus filled up quickly, meaning some of the old people eager to attend didn't have a seat. Chris received a heated phone call from Karrayili. 'You need to sort this out, now!'

The day of the wedding dawned dark, precipitating a last-minute change to the reception plans. It was supposed to be held on the lawn of the Mangrove Hotel under fairy lights and tossing palms with a view of the evening blues of Roebuck Bay. Instead, the cyclone pushed the party inside. According to Chris, this was a blessing. 'It provided a distraction from the normal pandemonium of the wedding. We were making sure everyone had candles and torches, people could sit wherever they wanted, and as the night went on, we were joined by people who hadn't even been invited to the wedding!'

Wayne and Chris's friend from Fitzroy Crossing, Maree, had recorded one of the love songs the old people had crooned on that long bus trip to the Tandanya Exhibition. With the permission of the old people, she played it at the wedding. Wayne's cousins, the Pigram Brothers, also kindly performed, playing harmonica, mandolin and guitar—their singular sound would one day become inseparable from the idea of Broome.

The party carried on until late in the night, while outside the tall glass windows of the hotel, Cyclone Chloe sent stinging sheets of cool and welcome rain across the bay.

* * *

The longer Wayne was at KALACC, the more acutely he became aware of a gap between Aboriginal customary law and Western law. In Fitzroy, people were still punished under customary law. If this happened, as far as the old people were concerned, the issue was over and there needn't be the involvement of police. The police, on the other hand, were saying tribal punishment went too far, that those doing the punishing should face criminal charges. Wayne recalls, 'Under these circumstances, no-one was allowed to talk about it. It didn't sound right to me that whitefella law should simply invalidate blackfella law.'

He'd been thinking a lot about this tension between two worlds, two ways of doing things and, particularly, the two systems of law. In addition to his work with KALACC, Wayne was undertaking an Associate Diploma of Community Management through Batchelor College in the Northern Territory. One of his lecturers suggested he consider the formal study of Western law by enrolling in a pre-law course. Wayne warmed to the idea. He knew that if Aboriginal people were to be empowered under Western law and were to be able to make systemic changes, then they needed to understand the kartiyas' system inside out.

Wayne's decision to study law came at a fortuitous time nationally. Three years earlier, in 1992, the landmark Mabo case had been decided, recognising the land rights of the Meriam people who were Traditional Owners of Murray Island in the Torres Strait. Six of the seven High Court judges ruled that Australia was not terra nullius, or 'land belonging to no-one', when European settlement occurred. This case paved the way for the *Native Title Act 1993*. The Act established a process for claiming native title over lands and waters in Australia, meaning that once native title was recognised, Aboriginal people legally had rights to camp, hunt, fish, use water, hold meetings and perform ceremonies on their traditional lands.

The process to gain native title was arduous, and it was this area of law that Wayne would eventually be drawn to. But for the time being, after resigning from KALACC, he focused on getting through the University of Western Australia's Aboriginal Pre-Law Program (in 1995) and then into Murdoch University.

Wayne and Chris's eldest child, Sara, was born in Wayne's first year of study at Murdoch. She'd been conceived in Fitzroy Crossing at the couple's second residence—a caravan on the banks of the river with couches and a television outside. Chris recalls, 'We must have been watching telly together when Wayne grabbed me and lifted me up onto a coffee table. He'd just spotted a black-headed python. All the old people said, *Ahh, it's a rai, looking for a baby*.'

Rai are spirit beings, connector spirits, that spread energy with and through country.

From thereon, Sara's totem was a black-headed python.

Many years later, in an affirmation letter to Sara in her final year of high school, the couple, reflecting on Sara's birth, wrote, 'What followed was a whirlwind of absolute exhaustion. We had never in our lives functioned on so little sleep. We knew nothing about looking after babies—someone had to show us how to do the cloth nappy and wrap you up. You wouldn't drink or sleep and you cried a lot! Thank goodness for Aunty Cassie (Wayne's youngest sister) living with us, we don't know how we would have survived without a little bit more help ... It wasn't long before you turned into a lovely toddler ...'

Wayne and Chris's second-born, Jarred, took his spirit from a barni—a goanna. On a hunting trip, Wayne had hit a barni with a distinct mark on its back. Jarred was born with a mirror-image of the same mark on his back. Tessa came third and her baby spirit was from Udialla, on the Martuwarra. This coincided with the family bringing in a big haul of silver barramundi. Barramundi became her spirit.

In Wayne's view, 'My job, as the father, was to find and capture a rai spirit for each of the children. I caught a barra, a barni and a snake. This means my kids have a responsibility to the land and to the Kimberley. They know their skin names, their bush names, their rai, things many Aboriginal young people may never know these days.'

* * *

On 31 January 2000—before Tessa had come along—Wayne had graduated with a law degree from Murdoch. There was still one more step before becoming a fully-fledged lawyer—Wayne needed to do his articles. He applied to BP, BHP, Rio Tinto and Shell but was unsuccessful, despite his grades sitting around credits and distinctions. He was knocked back by Legal Aid and Yamatji Marlpa Aboriginal Corporation. Feeling increasingly desperate, he contacted Yawuru man, former Kimberley Land Council director and now Labor senator Pat Dodson and asked his advice. Dodson suggested he call former politician turned QC Ian Viner. *Sure*, Ian told Wayne. *You can do your articles with me.*

Wayne's salary was twenty-four thousand dollars a year. 'It was a surreal life, walking around in Chambers on St Georges Terrace, wearing a suit and tie. It was like I was on a different planet, part of the grind for the legal fraternity, surrounded by incredible wealth and knowledge. I was a long way from carting fresh water to the house in buckets, using a generator for power, and heating up drums of water on the fire back in Derby to have a warm wash.'

Wayne was glad Ian took a chance on him. 'He taught me to understand legal issues and I thought about it this way—if you're trying to cut through the bone, and saw away, it's very difficult hard work. But you can slice easily through the joints. It's the same with legal issues; there's a certain skill in approaching and cutting through problems. Ian spent a lot of time mentoring me and giving me strategic experience, rather than just treating me like a workhorse, and for this I'm forever grateful.'

Wayne had the sense that he was doing a good job but after a couple of years, now with a different firm, he found himself becoming ruthless. 'I wasn't happy as a lawyer. It was all about winning and I was dealing with a number of matters that didn't feel right. I was representing clients against Aboriginal people, and people who were hard on their luck... I had become a lawyer because I had a sense of justice. I felt at the time what I was doing wasn't just.'

The couple were sick of the city and eager to get back to the Kimberley, back onto country and back working for the mob. When the KLC advertised for a chief executive officer, Wayne applied, and he landed the job. At only thirty-three years of age, he was set to lead one of the most powerful Aboriginal organisations in Australia. Wayne felt ready for the challenge. The years spent working for Ferdy had given him tenacity and stamina, his time as a lawyer in the city had hardened him, and his days in Fitzroy had earned him the cultural respect of the old people.

What he wasn't ready for—what the couple didn't, couldn't foresee—was that Wayne's acceptance of the position set the young family hurtling toward one of the most traumatic and testing times they would experience.

4: The frontline and the battleline

In his first few months as chief executive of the Kimberley Land Council, Wayne was merciless. He wanted an A-team around him. He became the firing squad.

'I believe I had a mandate from the members and the board to take the organisation to a different level and I needed to build a new team to help me do that. I told the middle management, *You either love working for this organisation, and you uphold its values, or you don't*. Those who didn't were moved on.'

Divina D'Anna, a Yawuru, Nimanburr and Bardi woman—then a young project officer, now Kimberley MP—was one of those who loved working for KLC, though she recalls Wayne's office style was 'an acquired taste'.

'Wayne would walk in and he wouldn't say good morning. You wouldn't get an acknowledgement. He was always on the phone, always talking business. I used to get wild with him but slowly came to understand the way his mind worked. You had to keep him focused. He would start talking about one issue, go right around and talk about something else, then come back to where he started.'

Wayne's mind was so agile, so quick, he often unravelled several threads of thought within the one conversation, demanding intense mental gymnastics from his listeners or staff. For Merrilee Williams, who served in various roles at KLC including as Wayne's executive assistant, these mental gymnastics were rarely prefaced with small talk. 'His wife, Chris, played a big role in teaching him to communicate with staff, to ask, *how are you?* and to check in with people. He appreciated what everyone did, he was grateful, he just had to learn to express it.'

Merrilee quickly grew to admire Wayne's approachability and drive. 'He'd come in with this raw, rippling energy ... He had the attitude that *Aboriginal people aren't pushovers, we're here, we've got a voice, and we can do this.* He would take the voice of Traditional Owners who wanted something, and then he would give their idea the dynamite to get it going. He always had time for his staff, even if it wasn't much time. *I've got five minutes*, he'd say, or *I've got two minutes before the next meeting.* His leadership style has always been to support others to succeed. He built me up like that.'

Winning the staff over was just the first part of the new job's challenge.

There was also the challenge of reinspiring KLC's membership. 'I travelled through the Kimberley to ascertain the views of everyone, to see what was going on. I spoke to all the non-believers, or anyone who wanted to talk to me. There were some negative rumours about KLC and its leadership, including that the Land Council was involved in corruption and improper dealings.' In Wayne's view, such rumours stemmed from trauma. 'People are victims of colonisation, they're disempowered. Aboriginal people, in an effort to survive, have developed protective strategies which mean they have become very suspicious of everyone and everything. This has become the norm, and they've had to do this in order to survive. The Land Council stood up for justice and a fair go, and KLC's leadership became a target.' Wayne—wary of the 'divide and conquer' tactics of governments, pastoralists and resource companies—knew there was power in having a single, mobilised and cohesive regional body that could fight for the rights and interests of Kimberley Traditional Owners.

This was particularly important in the grimly racist political climate. The prime minister at the time, John Howard, had wanted to make amendments to the *Native Title Act 1993* so it would give, in one commentator's view, 'cattle more rights than Indigenous people' (Bullimore 77). Howard had refused to apologise to the Stolen Generations and opposed the United Nation's Declaration on the Rights of Indigenous Peoples.

Wayne recalls, 'There was also a stigma around practising native title law. I was told, *Don't do native title because you'll become pigeonholed, you won't get enough experience as a good lawyer*. In those early years, I would advertise for a lawyer, and sometimes no-one would apply.'

Native title law was still relatively new and came about following the Mabo decision in 1992. If Traditional Owners were granted native title it meant, among other things, they may be able to live on their traditional land, visit and protect important sites, as well as access country for fishing, hunting and the gathering of food, medicine and other resources. The introduction of the Native Title Act caused a frenzy of fearmongering at the heart of which was the idea that people's homes would be in danger from native title claims. David Flint wrote in *The Australian* of the 'farmers and miners who have paid for Mabo, and are still paying …' and the *Sydney Morning Herald* carried the headline 'Fear of native title land grab in cities' (Flint 26, Peatling 5). One Nation leader Pauline Hanson claimed on radio station 2GB, 'a lot of people have been dispossessed of their lands in Australia because of it' (RMIT ABC).

In combatting these claims, senior Nyikina man John Watson said, 'We don't want to take Whitefeller's back yards or farms. We just want enough land to live in dignity, where our children can grow up with self-respect' (Fox 142).

John had borne the brunt of these attacks firsthand. His son, Anthony Watson, says upon the announcement of the introduction of the Native Title Act, his dad was threatened on his way to the shops in Derby. A whitefella said to him, *If anyone wants to take my land, I'll shoot you, I've got guns.*

Under Wayne's leadership, the KLC would grow to have two key functions: securing native title and negotiating agreements and land access. Wayne had been told by Merle Carter, a Gajerrong woman, that she'd seen the KLC as the warrior for Kimberley Aboriginal people, as the blackfella union. Wayne knew for the KLC to fulfil these two functions, and to properly represent its membership as a warrior, he needed to look to the past.

* * *

The Kimberley Land Council was formed at a bush meeting and dance festival on Noonkanbah Station in 1978. Eric Mjöberg, the Swedish bone thief, had passed through Noonkanbah sixty-eight years earlier, when white men ruled the homestead and Aboriginal men and women slaved over sheep. Now the station was operated and staffed by Traditional Owners—the people of the Yungngora community.

KLC's inaugural meeting drew over one thousand Aboriginal people from thirty Kimberley communities and five communities in the Northern Territory. The KLC of 1978 reported, 'On the first day of the meeting all the representatives of the different communities ... talked about their own situations and experiences and about the benefits they would get from joining together and sharing their common experience and making their voices one voice, and they decided yes, they would set up a Land Council. And so the KLC arrived' (KLC newsletter).

It would come to be governed and guided by a board of directors, cultural advisors and a chairperson, and it would be led by a chief executive officer.

One of the burning issues discussed at the meeting was that no type of land holding in Western Australia gave Aboriginal people ownership rights, or the right to control entry onto land. With a boom in oil and diamond exploration, Traditional Owners were concerned with impacts to their communities, land and sacred sites. Noonkanbah Station alone was quilted with around five hundred mining leases, including leases held by Amax, a multinational oil company headquartered in America.

While the meeting was underway Amax damaged a burial site, an ancient dancing ground, and the birthplace and tree containing the spirit of Friday Muller—the meeting's principal host. An anthropologist who'd seen the company's bulldozer peeling up the sandy floor of a popular swimming spot raced back to the meeting with news of the incursion, and a delegation of Traditional Owners was sent to investigate. They intercepted the bulldozer and one of the men, a visitor from the Northern Territory, knocked the driver's sunglasses from his face. He said if this had happened on his country, the driver would have been speared (Hawke and Gallagher 108).

The community of Noonkanbah fought from 1978 to 1980 to prevent Amax from drilling a wildcat well on their land. Amax's proposed activities fell within a whole complex of sacred sites around Umpampurra, or Pea Hill, and the community was appalled to learn there was only a one-in-fifty chance of the company finding oil or gas. They couldn't fathom why the state government was insisting on drilling at any cost, given the low probability of success and the certainty of further damage to sacred sites.

The community presented a petition to the Parliament of Western Australia, written in Walmajarri and translated into English, in which they eloquently expressed their views.

'These people have already made the place no good with their bulldozers. Our sacred places they have made no good. They mess up our land. They expose our sacred objects. This breaks our spirit. We lose ourselves as a people' (Yungngora Community).

* * *

The petition was ignored—the premier, Sir Charles Court, was out to make a point: Aboriginal people could not be seen to be obstructing development.

In one photo from the dispute, Premier Court appears in the Noonkanbah woolshed. He's towering over a group of seated old men, his hands on his hips. In another, Amax's chief executive, Tom Lyon, likewise talks down to a circle of seated men. Aviator sunglasses obscure his eyes. The body language of both men suggests arrogance, antagonism, even discomfort—qualities evident in the negotiations with Traditional Owners over the course of the dispute. The community and company found themselves in a deadlock between two laws: Aboriginal people were breaking white men's law by attempting to prevent drilling, and Amax was breaking Aboriginal law by drilling on sacred ground.

In one of the eeriest confrontations of the dispute, the old Lawmen, including a lightning man and rainmaker from Looma, conjured a storm which blew into the community from Amax's camp. Two days later, Aboriginal men from the community closed in on the drill site, bringing with them firewood, blocking the road, and setting up camp about a hundred metres from the police and contractors. At around nine that evening, two men with strong voices began to sing for a group of around one hundred dancers. Off to the side, a separate group of old men sang other songs—the secret songs of the Law and the land.

Steve Hawke, author of the history *Noonkanbah* and son of the former prime minister Bob Hawke, writes that it was a 'masterly piece of psychological warfare' (Hawke and Gallagher 210).

The contractors and police became unnerved. One of the pilots admitted that over the course of the night he went from 'being this great nationalistic Aussie, saying this was bad, Aussies being precluded from going about their business, to … saying, this is Amax's problem, not mine' (Hawke and Gallagher 212).

The next day Amax's contractors deserted, and the company pulled out temporarily. It was only a minor win: at the end of the story there were no winners. With the state government's blessing, backing and assistance, Amax went ahead and drilled its well on sacred ground.

It yielded nothing.

Premier Court's relentlessness was perhaps driven by a personal conviction that a prosperous future for the state hinged on mining development and by a desire to set a precedent ahead of what was shaping up to be a significant diamond discovery in the East Kimberley.

* * *

In the Dreamtime a female barramundi was chased into the shallow, muddy water of a cave by a group of women (Australian Human

Rights).⁹ The women prepared to ensnare her with their spinifex nets, but the barramundi leaped from the water, sailed over their heads and disappeared through a gap in the rocks. As she escaped, she lost some of her scales, which fell into the water and hardened to diamonds.

Fast forward to 1979, a year into the Noonkanbah dispute, and there were rumours that someone had been carving new roads into the country near Barramundi Gap. Initially it was thought to be cattle thieves, but it soon became apparent the roads belonged to the Ashton Joint Venture, managed by Conzinc Riotinto of Australia (CRA). CRA's exploration arm had found a giant cache of diamonds on the lands of the Miriuwung, Kija, Wularr and Malngin peoples.

Traditional Owners and the Kimberley Land Council pleaded with the joint venture to stop work, including around the Barramundi Dreaming site and another sacred site called Devil Devil Springs. Their pleas were ignored. The joint venture dismissed a KLC directive that all discussions with Traditional Owners be conducted through a properly representative negotiating team. Instead it dealt secretly with only one family group who spoke for the area. John Toby was the main spokesperson for the group. He'd initially alerted the KLC to the activities near his family's Glen Hill (Mandangala) outstation, concerned the activities might interfere with important sites. Eventually, he was flown to Perth along with several others to sign off on an agreement with the company. In a phone call to the KLC, Toby said, 'We've been beaten and we don't want to lose out the way people at Noonkanbah will. Been offered about $100,000 to begin with and payments for the life of the mine—that's the Mandangala family group—nothing for Warmun' (Skyring 2002).

The company promised to assist the family through payments tied to improvements on the station, such as the construction of fences, yards and buildings, upgrading the road and providing a few vehicles.

The KLC was critical of the process: legal representation was arranged at the last minute, discussions with Traditional Owners were held in secret, and a third party or representative body wasn't present. There was also the issue of gender—Barramundi Gap was a women's site and some women felt the joint venture didn't address gender as a significant factor in the original agreement. Other Traditional Owners advised CRA that the signatories to the agreement represented only an eighth of those whose lands the diamond mine would occupy. They said Toby did not speak for them. They refused to be bound by whatever the family had signed.

Six months later one of the signatories, Peggy Patrick, had a son crippled in an accident involving a truck provided to the community under the terms of the Glen Hill Agreement. While the company was quick to repair the truck, potential social impacts weren't factored into the original agreement. Neither were royalties, compensation or land rights.

When Rio Tinto began mining at Lake Argyle it virtually doubled world diamond production overnight. It became the world's largest producer of coloured diamonds—cognac and champagne, violet and pink. An Argyle pink diamond ring might fetch over eighty thousand dollars.

The Traditional Owners saw almost nothing of the vast, sparkling wealth being pried from their lands.

* * *

One of Wayne's first tasks at the helm of the KLC was to oversee the renegotiation of the Glen Hill Agreement in 2002. He did this with the guidance of Ciaran O'Faircheallaigh, a brilliant Irishman who was Australia's leading international scholar on interactions between Indigenous peoples and the mining industry. The two had met serendipitously during the tea-break of a mining, minerals and sustainable development conference. Ciaran told Wayne that Rio Tinto had asked him to help with the renegotiation. He said, 'I don't work for mining companies and I'm not too keen on the idea. But if something could be arranged jointly [with Traditional Owners *and* Argyle], I might be interested.' Wayne appreciated Ciaran's integrity and engaged him to deliver the first renegotiation workshop with the KLC and Argyle Diamonds.

From there, Ciaran became a key negotiator for the KLC.

Argyle was a pressure cooker situation for the young CEO. First, there were the tactics played by Argyle Diamond's management. In Wayne's view they got very personal, very micro, suggesting Wayne and the company were on the same level. 'There was an absolute game plan happening where I was brought closer and closer into the loop of friendship and trust. I thought I was managing it. But I reflect on it now and I say it wasn't genuine. Companies want you to think small and one of the strategies is to befriend you. When you're in a friendship it changes the relationship, especially when you're an Aboriginal person, because for us, there's not business friendship and personal friendship. Friendship is friendship. And this challenged those core values as to whether you can go hard on them. It was a psychological strategy Argyle ran to control negotiations. It wasn't personal—you've got to be a pretty tough and confident individual to drive negotiations.'

Ciaran recalls some frank conversations he had with the young CEO. 'On one occasion, Wayne arrived [at one of the negotiations] on a charter flight. I said to him, *You can't just fly in and fly out of these things.* I talked about the importance of understanding the company, which really resonated with Wayne. It's one of my strongest senses about Wayne as a person. He's fascinated by the way things work, whether that's a piece of machinery, or a big mining company … there's that mixture between being interested by the innards of things, and how they work, and being able to think about the big picture.'

In the early stages of the Argyle negotiations Wayne found himself struggling with his team. 'Ciaran pulled me aside and said, *Wayne, you need to make a decision, because you can't go on like this. You cannot do good deals if you're not happy with the performance of your team. You either have to move them on, or you need to understand what their issues are and put in place what's required to give them confidence.*'

Wayne considered Ciaran's advice. Given the complexity of the negotiations, an entirely new team wasn't an option. He recalled his KALACC days, in which the old people had lifted him up, supported him. It was now his turn to do the same with the people he was mentoring. He was also learning that when negotiating with 'all-powerful' companies like Argyle, a lot needed to be done to brief the team on history: the company's history, including its past engagement with Traditional Owners, and Aboriginal history. 'By teaching history, you can stoke the sense of the passion in your team that's required to get good deals. A good understanding of this history also sets the foundation for a plan and strategy for negotiations. As a representative of Traditional Owners, your job is to get them to think big. You provide good information so they can make good decisions and if companies fund this process, you can do deals within the timeframe. You bring expertise to the table so Traditional Owners can understand finance, environmental impacts and social impacts.

Without good information, Traditional Owners make poor decisions.'

A key issue for Wayne was that KLC was funded to achieve native title outcomes, not commercial outcomes. This meant the organisation had to rely on Rio Tinto's sense of corporate social responsibility for the additional funds to support the negotiations.

Communicating complex facets of the agreement-making was also a challenge. 'Financial literacy levels among the mob were low and we had to spend time breaking down information, like, what are percentages? What's confidentiality? We worked out ways to explain these things. When it came to percentages, we talked about catching a fish, or a kangaroo, and dividing it up. If you've got a kangaroo, you might split it four ways, taking a quarter for yourself and giving the other three quarters to your family.'

Wayne recalls Divina D'Anna likening the concept of confidentiality to a card game. 'We would tell everyone, *So, you know when you play cards, you don't show everyone the cards you've got in your hand, right? Because if everyone knows you've got good numbers, they'll fold. And that's not good for you, because they haven't put any money on the table. Confidentiality is holding your cards close until it's the right time to put them down, and show everyone, because you might just have the winning hand*.'

Throughout the negotiations, Wayne and his team pushed for a broad range of economic, social and community benefits in exchange for the expansion of the diamond mine. The renegotiated agreement included the landmark clause 'no means no'. This was crucial because it accepted the principle that the company couldn't damage any sites without Traditional Owner consent. Without this clause, if Traditional Owners said no to development, companies and the government could simply overrule them. 'No means no' also meant if Traditional Owners wanted work stopped because it threatened cultural heritage, the company would have to stop work until the issue was resolved.

The final Argyle agreement set the benchmark; it laid the architecture for all Kimberley agreements going forward. This architecture would continue to be built on, to be strengthened. In Wayne's view, 'When you look at past agreements, you always know you can make them better.'

* * *

During the renegotiation, Wayne and Ciaran formed a friendship which then strengthened over the next two decades. The scholar admired the way the young Aboriginal leader conducted himself in meetings. Ciaran had sat in on Traditional Owner negotiations where leaders had walked out. 'Wayne would never do this. If there's a problem, he works it out ... I would describe him as someone who is a careful and deep thinker, who combines that with a keen practical sense. He has very strong cultural ties and is really focused on making a difference.'

The two also worked together on an agreement relating to the reopening of the Koolan Island iron ore mine with the Dambimangari people in 2003, the Tanami Gold mining agreement with Tjurabalan native title holders, and the Browse Agreements for the proposed gas plant at James Price Point. Each agreement raised the bar higher when it came to Aboriginal employment and the protection of cultural heritage. Ciaran observed one of the things that made KLC's agreement-making capacity so impressive was its ability to engage in political, legal and technical arenas—a difficult or impossible feat for individual groups of Traditional Owners.

Wayne says that the 'KLC had been set up as an organisation with cultural authority, it was a grassroots organisation, it was the people's organisation, it was the voice of the people'.

As a statutory native title representative body, KLC also had to work within governmental and judicial systems. During Wayne's ten years as chief executive he oversaw the successful native title determination of close to seventy percent of the Kimberley. In 2003 the KLC was working on nearly one third of Australia's native title claims. At the same time it was still an advocacy group and was active in criticising government to achieve better policy outcomes for Kimberley Aboriginal people.

Throughout his early years at the KLC, Wayne followed with interest the careers of many Aboriginal leaders, including Noel Pearson, Marandoo Yanner, Patrick Dodson and Peter Yu. He admired the pressure they put on governments to improve the lot of Aboriginal people.

'I looked up to them as incredible Aboriginal leaders. I don't think people realised the sacrifices they made. The endless hours away from family. The endless hours travelling. Living out of a suitcase. Arguing with politicians to improve the well-being and social justice outcomes of Aboriginal people. Change in Aboriginal affairs has always been incremental and it's hard to see that kind of change. Sometimes, when you're just looking forward, you can't see the dots and how they join. When you look back, you see their advocacy has joined a lot of dots. We've seen improvements in funding for Aboriginal housing, Aboriginal education and Aboriginal health. This is because of their collective pressure over time. They put pressure on governments to do something. In the case of Pat Dodson and Peter Yu, they were the founders of the modern movement which provided the basis to elevate KLC as an advocate for rights and justice in the Kimberley. They set up the policy platform for change.'

* * *

A year into the job, aged thirty-four, Wayne was asked by a journalist: Do Aboriginal people get special treatment? He told the journalist, 'My grandparents were Stolen Generation. My people are overly represented in every negative statistic—in health, education, prisons. That's the special treatment Aboriginal people get' (Dick 9).

But just as social justice was a motivating factor in Wayne's work, so was a desire to walk in two worlds, as both a strong cultural man and a participant in the modern economy. He was inspired, in part, by the famed and feared North American Apache leader Geronimo. Ciaran had gifted Wayne a copy of Geronimo's biography. Within its pages Wayne encountered a warrior with a reputation so fierce he was said to wear a blanket stitched from one hundred human scalps. While this was fiction, Geronimo led many successful raids into Mexico, fought hard to guard his traditional lands, and was the last Native American warrior to concede to United States forces. He was described as alternately arrogant and generous, humble and proud; a man who was not a liar but who would use deception for strategic purposes; a man who felt, in his later years, as though his own people had turned from him. He was square shouldered, deep chested and well dressed. What Wayne most admired about Geronimo's story was his capacity to walk in two worlds. 'Geronimo was loved and loathed. He was very cultural, but not afraid to make a go of it in the white man's world. Once he realised he was beaten, he adopted the Western system and died very wealthy…' Geronimo was shrewd in his approach to a traditional cultural economy by supporting his family and providing for his people through hunting and raiding. He was also shrewd in his approach to the Western economy. He banked the money he acquired as a Wild West exhibit and set up a profitable souvenir-selling business. When artists and writers requested permission to paint him or to tell his story, he charged them for the privilege. Here was a man who embodied how two different cultural ways of seeing, knowing and living might be possible, even compatible.

Concurrent to these developments in Wayne's own thinking, there were also new developments within his family. As Wayne and Chris's two youngest grew a little older, it became apparent to Chris their children were autistic. The more she read about it, the more she realised Wayne, too, displayed many autistic characteristics.

Wayne says it was his lack of social awareness that may have saved him from a complete breakdown during his time at the helm of the KLC. 'When people ran me down, or criticised me, I never responded because I didn't pick up on it. I'd take things literally, miss the innuendo. I used to bring people into meetings with me to read the tension in the room. We'd go outside every so often so they could let me know what was happening on an emotional level in the meetings. It probably allowed me to last as long as I did, to feel comfortable seeing and meeting up with all my enemies, all my non-believers.'

This extra armour would be particularly useful in the battle ahead. So would Wayne's approach to fighting for the rights of Traditional Owners.

5: Every strong life calls forth enemies

Two hundred billion dollars worth of gas was entombed just offshore from Broome. It was deep. Difficult to extract. And processing was an issue. Potential options included piping it a thousand kilometres to existing plants in the Pilbara, processing it on a floating facility or building a gas plant on the Kimberley coast.

Wayne was aware several proponents were angling to build a gas plant on the coast, including Inpex, a Japanese company which favoured the Maret Islands in the north Kimberley for its forty-year project. The islands were on the secluded lands of the Wunambal Gaambera people and had been traditionally used for fishing, turtle hunting, and ceremonies. KLC, representing the Uungurr native title group, battled to get Inpex to the table. The company said it wasn't affecting native title rights and interests because it was drilling in the water. KLC flew Traditional Owners over the islands and, following an aerial inspection of the company's worksite, wrote to the WA minister for the environment, requesting an assessment of the cultural values of the area. The minister said Inpex would need to apply for a licence under Section 91 of the *Land Administration Act 1997*—this could be granted without Traditional Owner consent. In response, KLC demanded the company negotiate a heritage agreement before it proceeded any further.

Wayne recalls, 'It wasn't so much an instance of a company trying to evade responsibility, but more an instance of the way the state government applied the law.'

Eventually a dialogue commenced between the two parties. KLC facilitated negotiations, and by 2007 the Uungurr native title group entered into a suite of preliminary agreements with Inpex involving heritage protection, flora and fauna studies, and a negotiation protocol.

But Inpex wasn't the only company interested in the Browse Basin gas fields.

In 2004 Woodside Petroleum Ltd appointed an ambitious Nebraskan, Don Voelte, as its chief executive. Voelte loved hunting and car racing and had decades of experience in global oil and gas. He drew on the latter to refresh a resistant and lethargic team, making it clear to his staff that 'you are either on the bloody train, or under the bloody train' (Klinger).

Voelte's train was accelerating fast.

Woodside approached KLC to outline their plans for a gas-processing facility on the Dampier Peninsula north of Broome. The Peninsula was home to an estimated fifteen hundred predominantly Aboriginal people, who accessed their communities via a road of red-dirt corrugations. Nestled among species of grevillea and melaleuca were clinics, schools and Aboriginal-run tourism ventures, as well as a pearl farm at Cygnet Bay, a trochus hatchery and the old Beagle Bay Mission. It was here on the Peninsula that Wayne's great-grandmother Jira had been taken, his Nana Aggie had grown up, his maternal grandfather had been born, and his Uncle Cyril now lived. Agnes Bryan Guilwill, Wayne's great-grandmother (Thomas Puertollano's mother), was a Nyul Nyul woman from that country. A remnant from the old mission, the Sacred Heart Church, drew shoals of tourists who came to admire its gleaming altar of pearl, cowry, volute and olive snail shells. Yoolya had helped to build the church; Nana Aggie had been married in it.

Woodside and KLC jointly undertook community consultations to gauge how receptive Traditional Owners on the Peninsula were to the proposition of a gas plant. Traditional Owners weren't receptive. In 2005 Woodside held a meeting of its own with a group of senior men at Mudnunn. The outcome was a resounding 'no' from senior cultural leaders. Wayne didn't attend. He believed KLC was being undermined and Traditional Owners disrespected. He had already indicated to Woodside that the senior men were not keen on the project at that time.

A few weeks later Wayne's phone started ringing with reports that Woodside and representatives from the state government were poking around on the Dampier Peninsula to gauge Traditional Owner appetite for a gas hub. Wayne heard the head of State Development was visiting Traditional Owners over a long weekend. He heard that Aboriginal people who were not Traditional Owners from that area were consulting on behalf of Woodside.

Each time he picked up the phone, the warning bells tolled louder.

'I became alarmed. I felt like the control of these decisions was about to be taken out of the hands of Traditional Owners. I felt like we needed a proper consultation process in place. It was important the state and developers directed their discussions through KLC.'

For Wayne there was an uncomfortable echo here of the circumstances surrounding the original Glen Hill Agreement, in which Rio Tinto had sidestepped KLC to negotiate directly with Traditional Owner family representatives. The result was profoundly damaging to relationships and cultural heritage, and financially detrimental to the Traditional Owners. The establishment of the giant iron ore mines of the 1960s in the Pilbara was also on Wayne's mind, as was the *North West Gas Development (Woodside) Agreement Act 1979*. It was apparent Woodside was proposing a major development and, unless KLC stepped in, Traditional Owners might lose the opportunity to insist on the protection of cultural and heritage values and to participate in responsible development.

'I was concerned with the question: how were we as a people to get ahead? Why was it okay for those in mainstream society to build an economic base, but when it came to us, if we built an economic base, we were not real Aboriginal people? Coming from Mangkaja Arts, we'd always asked government, or wealthy philanthropists, for help, which is a form of soft economic power. *Help us get a job! Help me sell my art!* I realised we had to mix it up. We no longer wanted to rely on others for help. We had to create some wealthy Aboriginal organisations, and wealthy Aboriginal people, so we could shape our own future, on our own country.'

Wayne saw a chance, maybe a once-in-a-lifetime chance, to do what governments had failed to do for decades—to lift his people out of poverty. His people could expect to live for twenty years less than non-Indigenous people. They were less likely to own their own homes. They were more likely to take their own lives.

So, *if* gas development was guided by Aboriginal people, *if* Aboriginal people had direct authority over the money with good advice, *if* the whole process was negotiated in a culturally appropriate way consistent with aarnja—a system of local and regional governance which provides a cultural basis for benefit sharing— then it might serve to do what decades of government funding had been unable to. It might help to improve the lives of all Kimberley Aboriginal people. Wayne reflects, 'Aboriginal kids could choose to live in a [remote] community lifestyle or work on the business strip of St Georges Terrace in Perth. *This* would be intergenerational change.'

But it would only be possible if Kimberley Aboriginal people spoke up.

Only if Kimberley Aboriginal people took control.

* * *

Not long after Woodside was knocked back by the senior men, Wayne was on the Dampier Peninsula for a meeting relating to secret men's evidence for the Bardi Jawi native title trial. 'We had all the senior men there, including Joseph Roe, Paul Sampi and Frank Davey. I said, *We need to stop what's happening, with individual people running around. If we continue to allow uncontrolled engagement with mining companies, without following a protocol, the message is going to be undermined.* I asked the men what they wanted to do about the gas consultations. They agreed we should engage together, and that information needed to be transparent. Everyone needed to be able to access good information and advice to make informed decisions. We would go back to Woodside and determine a location by talking with all coastal groups in the Kimberley, not just those on the Peninsula.'

'I took a group of senior men down to Perth and we met Don Voelte. There was this incredible contrast between the glitz and glamour and ritz of Perth, and the other way we do business, which is sitting under shady trees and feeling the sand in our fingers. We had dinner in one of Woodside's executive rooms and encouraged the company to engage with us properly.'

The state government was supportive of formal engagement.

In June 2007 it established the Northern Development Taskforce (NDT) to 'identify suitable possible locations for at least one gas processing complex which would be used to process Browse Basin gas' ('Northern Development Taskforce to Guide'). The taskforce would also help craft a vision for the long-term future of the Kimberley. According to the treasurer and minister for state development, Eric Ripper, it was important that 'any sites that are identified have the informed consent of the traditional owners, and that significant benefits can flow from the Browse Basin gas project to the broader Aboriginal community in the region' (Northern Development Taskforce – Browse). The state also entered into a financial support agreement with KLC to enable it to consult and engage with Traditional Owners along the length of the Kimberley coast.

For KLC the first step was to hold a series of meetings with fifteen initial coastal claim groups that might be affected by the development of a gas hub.[10] Wayne and his staff travelled thousands of kilometres in troopies and small planes. By night they slept in swags, safari tents, dongas and motels; by day they delivered speeches and handed out detailed information so groups were made aware of the interest in Browse and could begin to weigh the benefits against the drawbacks of hosting a gas plant on their country.

Divina D'Anna remembers Wayne talking to each group about the ripple effect—if you threw a rock into a waterhole, the ripples would spread all over. Similarly, if big development occurred in the Kimberley, the ripples would spread all over and might include pressures on housing, the environment, or new roads opening up people's country. The other metaphor Divina remembers Wayne using was that of the sticks. 'He would say, *Look, if you've got one stick, you can easily break it. But if you get all the sticks together, like this, it's harder to break them. That's what we need to do. We need to stand together.* He used metaphors to really ensure those old people on the ground understood what was happening.'

Each group elected four representatives to be on a Traditional Owner Task Force. They became the contact point for questions and information about gas development, making recommendations on sharing benefits, and participating in consultations. According to Wayne, 'Aboriginal decision-making was a matter for each group. There were groups who made decisions in accordance with traditional laws and customs, and there were groups whose elders said it was okay first and then they put it to the whole group to say "yes" or "no" by way of a vote. In some cases relating to the assessment of location, one or two elders said no, and then that was the end of the assessment; everyone followed that decision.'

Opponents would later query the seven million dollars the state government gave KLC to undertake these consultations. There were allegations the money was used to buy Traditional Owner consent. Sceptics wondered how KLC could act in the interest of Indigenous people if they were being funded by a state government eager to pursue its own agenda.

As far as Wayne was concerned, Traditional Owners were given no recognition of their proprietary rights and as such had to accept the dollars. 'What was the alternative? If we didn't play the game of chess, if we didn't accept the resources from the state, we wouldn't have been able to run the consultations and we wouldn't have been able to give the best possible information and advice to the groups to make informed decisions. It also allowed us to engage advisors. The state government had oil and gas advisors. Woodside was hiring advisors to help with Indigenous engagement … Aboriginal people were being asked to make complicated decisions with no advisors of our own. We needed independent advice and the state's funding allowed us to provide this.'

As consultations began, Wayne became troubled with another issue. What if development got out of hand? What if there were multiple gas plants—perhaps a concrete choker of gas plants—fastened around the neck of the Kimberley coast?

In December 2007, KLC, along with Environs Kimberley Inc., the World Wildlife Fund Australia, the Australian Conservation Foundation, the Wilderness Society of WA Inc. and the Conservation Council of Western Australia, released a joint position statement in which a set of principles was agreed upon to guide culturally and environmentally responsible gas development. The groups acknowledged the potential for beneficial outcomes for Traditional Owners from LNG and associated development. They called for a regional LNG plan that maximised the sharing of infrastructure and minimised the environmental footprint. And, critically, they championed a *single* gas hub—its establishment conditional on informed consent from Traditional Owners.

When the statement was released, the conservation groups didn't celebrate. There had been compromise to reach this position, ground had been ceded. But there was also a sense that it was the ethical thing to do at that moment in time, a way to manage the tension between a serious environmental threat and Traditional Owners' right to make decisions about their land.

The call for a single hub was accepted by the state government. The Northern Development Taskforce drafted a list of viable locations, considering cultural, financial and engineering factors. On 4 July 2008 the NDT released an interim report that identified eleven potential sites for evaluation; this was then whittled down to four: James Price Point, Gourdon Bay, Anjo Peninsula or North Head (*Northern Development Taskforce, Part A*). Throughout the process, if a group didn't want a gas plant on their country, they could opt out at any time. Wayne advised each of the four remaining groups, 'If you want to get off the list, you must get off now.'

At this stage, after an on-country consultation, Karajarri withdrew Gourdon Bay from the list.

This left three potential sites.

* * *

In order to fully visualise the impact of a gas plant on country, and to ensure Traditional Owners had all the information necessary to make the best possible decision, around forty people from the Traditional Owner taskforce travelled south in June 2008 to visit Woodside's hydrocarbon processing facility on the Burrup Peninsula. A year later, a smaller group travelled to the Petronas Bintulu LNG Complex in Sarawak, Malaysia. Recalling the Burrup trip, Irene Davey, a KLC cultural advisor and elected representative for Bardi Jawi, says she was shocked when she first set eyes on the plant. 'Goodness me,' she thought. 'It's going to be big, and it's going to take a lot of country. I said to a couple of the other Traditional Owners, *You can just imagine a person lying there. The pipes look like someone's intestines!*'

* * *

Up until this point, there had been genuine goodwill and a good working relationship between KLC and the state government. But Wayne still had his guard up. He knew that while Aboriginal leaders in the Kimberley might not change for decades, non-Aboriginal leaders, whether they were in government or the private or not-for-profit sectors, did change, often, moving sideways or upwards in pursuit of new career opportunities. Since the burgeoning interest in the Browse Basin, Wayne had already worked with two different state premiers and two different prime ministers.

When the Labor government led by Alan Carpenter called a shotgun election for 6 September 2008, Wayne braced himself for yet another change. Carpenter was facing off against Colin Barnett's Liberal opposition. At the previous election, Barnett had ambitiously campaigned to build a canal from the Kimberley to Perth, which would funnel water to the thirsty city. It was an unpopular idea, with analysts speculating it had contributed to the party's election loss. This election, Barnett promised to introduce tougher drug laws, boost regional hospital services and build schools across the state. There was no mention of the canal.

The Liberals won.

And with the incoming government came the collapse of the formerly established goodwill.

* * *

Two and a half weeks after the election, Inpex shelved its plans for a gas processing plant on the Maret Islands. This wasn't a surprise—the company had warned the chair of the Northern Development Taskforce that a number of the shortlisted sites were not suitable, particularly North Head due to the threat to whales. However, it also wasn't the authoritative start Premier Barnett might have hoped for. Inpex would have helped rekindle the languishing economy, and in the new premier's view, its withdrawal was 'the most embarrassing episode in the state's history' (Laurie 13). He blamed Traditional Owners, asserting they'd made exorbitant claims about how much they might get out of the project and accusing Carpenter's government of giving Traditional Owners veto over site selection ('Barnett Blames').

Wayne was incensed.

How could Traditional Owners be held solely responsible for a company building a multi-billion-dollar gas plant in the Northern Territory rather than in Western Australia?

'It is absolutely absurd for him [Barnett] to bash Aboriginal people,' he told ABC's *Stateline* ('Fallout Continues').

Inpex was lost, but Premier Barnett was determined to hang on to Woodside. Moving swiftly, he pared back the functions of the Northern Development Taskforce so it would work exclusively on site selection, and he threatened to seize the land through compulsory acquisition if Traditional Owners were unable to decide on a site.

In Wayne's view, the threat of compulsory acquisition was a gift to the environmentalists. They could walk away from their commitment to a single hub. Environs Kimberley, one of the signatories to the joint position statement, chose this moment to withdraw its support.

For Traditional Owners it wasn't a gift. It was a gun to the head.

* * *

On 17 October, pre-empting the Northern Development Taskforce process, Premier Barnett announced that of the four final locations on the list, he preferred North Head, near Beagle Bay. Kimberley MLA Carol Martin—Wayne's old next-door neighbour and welfare officer from Derby—said she thought James Price Point was most suitable. The Broome Chamber of Commerce and Industry also weighed into the debate, picking James Price Point and nominating North Head as its second choice. It dismissed the Anjo Peninsula altogether on the grounds that it was too far out of Broome and local businesses would miss out. Wayne saw the Chamber as taking a 'self-serving, self-interested position, to have it located in their shire'. The Anjo Peninsula, an old World War II site, was the only location Traditional Owners had provided conditional consent for from the outset. It was also, from a technical and engineering perspective, the best possible location.

Then, in another shock move, the premier changed his mind. In December 2008 he announced a gas plant wouldn't be built at North Head but at James Price Point, about sixty kilometres north of Broome. At a face-to-face meeting with Barnett in Perth, Wayne begged him to reconsider Anjo. 'But the premier said no. By doing so, he created the perfect storm …'

Into this storm KLC threw open an umbrella—a submission in response to the Northern Development Taskforce's *Site Evaluation Report Part B*. The submission outlined a profound concern: there were gaps in the information Traditional Owners needed to complete a site selection process. There was a lack of detail around development plans and activities, and no articulation of impacts on Indigenous people, heritage and culture. These gaps undermined KLC's commitment to world's best practice when it came to guiding responsible development.

The premier's announcement of James Price Point gave a concrete target to the project's opposition. There were concerns that a gas plant's light would extinguish the stars, dredging would disrupt dugong habitats, and carbon dioxide and benzene would poison the air. The old-world charm of Broome and Derby would be tainted, with the towns turning into hotspots for a 'careless itinerant' workforce (Vaughan 12). Broome's fishing community envisaged pressure on fish stocks from cashed-up oil and gas miners. Others worried about the cost of living, damage to the tourism industry and an exacerbation of the town's homelessness crisis. More frightening still was Barnett's broader dream of creating cities in the state's north modelled on Dubai (Forrest Backs). For many, this seemed more like a nightmare.

* * *

According to the premier, James Price Point, known locally as Walmadany, was 'a tableland. Flat as a table. An unremarkable beach. There are no cliffs, there are no hills, there are no communities probably within 30–40 kilometres. It is not the Kimberley that Qantas uses for its ads. Nothing like it' (Manning).

Anti-gas lobbyists were startled.

Was the premier blind? No cliffs? There were magnificent cliffs, which blazed the colour of blood oranges in the setting sun. And the area was remarkable for the density of dinosaur footprints and its major ethnographic and archaeological significance—its midden, artefacts and burial sites harboured over ten thousand pieces of material (Bradshaw and Fry). Above the high-tide line, sand dunes pillowed the bones of old people, and endangered monsoon vine thickets were home to wallabies, bats, bowerbirds and fruit-doves.

The area was at the heart of the Goolarabooloo's Lurujarri Heritage Trail, a coastal tourism track of over seventy kilometres which was initiated in the late 1980s by a gifted and multilingual storyteller called Paddy Roe (Heritage Trail). Paddy saw an opportunity to help educate non-Aboriginal Australians about Aboriginal sites and relationships to land. Like Wayne, he was Nyikina, born on Roebuck Plains Station around 1912. Like Wayne's great grandfather Yoolya, Paddy's mixed heritage made him a target for police. He tells of an instance when, upon seeing police approaching, his mum bundled him up in her swag and sat lightly on top. The police didn't suspect anything. Her quick thinking left Paddy to grow up fluent in both traditional culture and western station work. As a young man he fell in love with another man's wife, and the couple eloped to Jabirr Jabirr country. Here they were welcomed by several senior people who went on to make Paddy a custodian of their law, culture, songs and stories. 'Goolarabooloo' would come to be the term used to refer to Paddy's descendants and their claim for native title. However, while considered traditional custodians, the Goolarabooloo were not Traditional Owners for Jabirr Jabirr country, a fact formally established by the Federal Court in 2017. Native title law recognises those who have ancestral connections to country and can prove a continuing connection to country since British sovereignty. The Goolarabooloo had occupied the country for less than a hundred years. When Joseph Roe, Paddy's grandson, made a native title claim over the area on behalf of Goolarabooloo families in 1994, Jabirr Jabirr people wrote to the National Native Title Tribunal that they were the Traditional Owners for that country and while they were 'happy to work cooperatively with Goolarabooloo in this claim, they did want their rights in the country recognised' (*Roe* 123). The claim was thus amended and became a joint claim shared by the two groups.

In January 2009, eight years after his grandfather passed away, Joseph Roe, a named applicant who had been 'cautiously supportive of the gas precinct being located on his land' began to publicly and passionately rail against Woodside's proposal (Spencer 13). His charisma, intensity and willingness to engage with the media made him a compelling spokesman under whom non-Aboriginal anti-gas protesters rallied. Protesters and the media hailed Joseph as a 'law boss' for the area.

Within the Jabirr Jabirr group there were also those who were feeling increasingly uncomfortable about the project. Wayne saw their concerns as valid but knew KLC, as a native title representative body, had a mandate to work within native title law.

'At the end of the day, we had to take direction from the majority of the native title claim group. The majority of the group was eager to pursue negotiations and to find a balance between social, cultural and environmental values.'

As the wider Kimberley community grappled with KLC's role, the question was raised: how did KLC choose the position that it would lobby for a gas plant? Why wasn't it representing the views of those opposed to a gas plant—for example, those from other groups on the Dampier Peninsula?

Wayne understood the frustration, understood there were Aboriginal people with generational attachments to certain areas—members of his own family, like Yoolya, Jira and Gypsy (Jira's sister), had grown up a long way from Nyikina country. Many people had been taken to Beagle Bay Mission after being stolen, and they had come to know and love the country, to feel a deep historical connection to it. But Wayne's role as chief executive was to uphold the rights of Traditional Owners. 'It's the common law native title holders, or claimants, who have a property right based on their ancestral connections to country and it's their view that's taken account of. If people who don't have native title rights oppose this, then there are legal processes they can follow to have their voices heard.'

KLC was in a difficult position. Traditional Owners had no legal veto under native title law, and Wayne was chilled when he thought about what a worst-case scenario might look like. Should Traditional Owners refuse to negotiate, they would likely receive nothing—no jobs, no royalties, no protection of cultural heritage, no environmental safeguards that went above statutory requirements, no regional social benefits and no guarantee that the company would rehabilitate the area when operations were finally finished decades later. And if the agreement was rushed, Kimberley Traditional Owners might end up short-changed like some groups in the Pilbara—left with shattered cultural sites and poisoned water, left in poverty while mining companies drained millions of dollars from their lands each year. He'd encouraged Traditional Owners to watch *Exile and the Kingdom*, a film developed with several Aboriginal groups in the Pilbara that depicted the bleak reality of being excluded from mining agreements, a reality rife with unemployment, prostitution, alcoholism and poverty. In December 2008, Wayne sought the support of the federal minister for Indigenous affairs, Jenny Macklin, with an increasingly impatient premier. As a result of the meeting with Jenny Macklin, Barnett soon imposed a deadline on the parties, demanding that an in-principle heads of agreement which would guide the development be negotiated within three months. Throughout January 2009 traditional law business was taking place and non-Aboriginal staff were on leave. This left only two months—too quick for such a giant project.

* * *

The anti-gas lobby was also heating up. In January 2009, local musician and blacksmith Wil Thomas wrote to the *Broome*

Advertiser, 'People flock here from all over the world to see... untouched beauty. Why? Pretty simple really; because there's none left where they come from' (Thomas). A month earlier, Australian musician Missy Higgins, for whom Broome had long been a magic and creative space, said, 'We can't just sit back and let the oil and gas companies come and destroy this beautiful, beautiful land' ('Missy').

In just a few months, the protest movement became highly visual. 'No Gas' banners were strung up around town and across the front fences of people's homes. A cardboard box appeared on a roundabout reading: *Garage Sale. 'Prices Point'. Whales, Culture, Heritage, Beauty, Environment. Everything must go. Be quick* (Hingston). Carol Martin, who initially favoured James Price Point as a location, pulled up at her Broome office one morning to find a sign strung between two palm trees, calling her 'Carol Martian' and asking what planet she was from. Out of town, up at James Price Point, a group of protesters shed their undies and flaunted bum cheeks painted with letters that formed the slogan 'No gas on the Kimberley coast'.

The strength of the anti-gas lobby could perhaps be partly credited to its multifaceted nature. There wasn't just a single group that galvanised in opposition—single groups are easier to define, easier to attack, easier to dismiss. Instead, there were many groups: Environs Kimberley, Save The Kimberley, Protect the Kimberley, Hands off Country, and Families of Broome. And the protesters weren't simply a throng of 'bludgers ... liars, tree-huggers, blow-ins or ferals' as one Jabirr Jabirr gas opponent noted (Prior 'Aboriginal Protesters'). Among their ranks were local professionals of all ages and people representing the many different cultures of Broome. There were those who worked closely with Traditional Owners and supported Traditional Owner aspirations, but who were appalled by a state government that seemed to walk hand in hand with industry and horrified at the prospect of a planet-polluting gas plant in their backyard. The protesters campaigned hard to stall the project, in the hope that each delay would damage the state government's reputation, hurt Woodside's hip pocket and make a gas plant so expensive that Woodside and its joint venture partners would pull out altogether.

Irene Davey—who had been on the Traditional Owner Task Force—was related to several of the outspoken Aboriginal opponents of the gas plant. As the protest movement swelled, she was distraught at the impact on local Aboriginal families.

'The non-Aboriginal protesters didn't know the Jabirr Jabirr people had connections through that country. People were thinking about damage to country but not about the damage they were doing to the relationships within the tribe. I felt really saddened about the things that were said to people—how the protesters acted was awful. Aboriginal people needed to be able to say "no" and it meant "no". Or they needed to be able to say "yes" and then to follow through with good intentions. We got involved with this because we wanted a better future for our kids and the next generation.'

For Irene, it wasn't about the dollars.

* * *

Woodside made an initial offer of a benefits package worth two hundred million dollars to Traditional Owners to proceed with the development. The KLC refused to accept, stating it would take Indigenous compensation back three decades. With his usual flair for making complex issues visual, Wayne illustrated with a measuring tape why KLC was refusing. At a meeting with representatives from the state government and Woodside, KLC rolled out two hundred metres of tape in a tropical park on the edge of Roebuck Bay. 'So, this project is worth two hundred billion dollars,' Wayne said, addressing the crowd. 'Each metre represents a billion dollars.' He stepped out Woodside at one hundred and forty metres, then the Commonwealth—who stood to benefit through the Petroleum Resource Rent Tax—at nearly sixty metres. 'Now,' Wayne said. 'You have offered twenty centimetres to Traditional Owners.' He stepped on the tape at twenty centimetres and asked, 'Does that look fair to you? Doesn't look fair to me.'

* * *

Wayne was anxious about the rising tension among Traditional Owners. At KLC's AGM the year before, in October 2008, he'd called an impromptu meeting in an attempt to address concerns people had about the gas. But the impromptu meeting clashed with the time allocated for the Kimberley Language Resource Centre's AGM.[11] 'How dare you do this!' he was told by one Traditional Owner. 'Our language meeting is important.' The situation escalated: grievances were trumpeted, tempers soared and the crisis was only defused when one old person spoke up to defend the process and the need to give it time to be sorted.

Faced with the ticking bomb of compulsory acquisition, Wayne was grateful for the support of the federal minister for Indigenous affairs, Jenny Macklin. Macklin had committed funds to assist with the negotiation of the heads of agreement. A negotiation committee was created—of which Paddy Roe's grandson Joseph was a part—and numerous meetings were held to work out the finer details.

KLC enlisted two oil and gas experts to help with negotiations, one of whom was Cameron Syme. Syme, a lawyer and tough negotiator, assisted Wayne and Traditional Owners to broker a strong agreement in which the WA Government and Woodside would be required to fulfil a range of obligations. These obligations included working with the KLC and native title claimants on the co-design, construction, operation, decommission and rehabilitation of the site; a compensation package that went well beyond a cursory acknowledgement of native title rights and interests; a commitment to establish a regional benefits fund; and a commitment to grant Traditional Owners freehold land—a form of tenure much stronger than native title. Should Traditional Owners vote in favour of the agreement, then it would provide a basis from which the development of detailed Indigenous land use agreements could begin.

Gas opponents, like founding host of the ABC's *Foreign Correspondent* George Negus, declared Indigenous Australians shouldn't have to sell their souls, land and culture to reap economic benefits other Australians take for granted. Former Federal Court judge, the late Justice Murray Wilcox, echoed these sentiments, asking why Aboriginal people should 'sacrifice' country and culture for benefits other Australians receive as a right (Wilcox). Broadly, they were concerns Wayne shared. 'The Commonwealth should pay for those things, but the reality is different. Unless you have some sort of power to ensure that money is spent where smaller populations live, then the regions are often overlooked. The other point here is that Aboriginal people should be in charge of spending Aboriginal money—we should decide where the money goes.' The heads of agreement was a step toward giving Aboriginal people this control. What Wayne took issue with was Wilcox's use of the word 'sacrifice'. 'It sets up a different language of talking about Indigenous rights. We don't talk about Australian citizens "sacrificing" their land. The use of the word "sacrifice" demonises and tarnishes the notions of goodwill and informed consent.'

He also took issue with the way the media was covering the protest. 'The media was putting people up as law bosses, elders, Traditional Owners. The short, punchy grabs journalists used in their news reports were in direct conflict with the proper process to ensure an authentic, authorised Indigenous voice. We had spent huge amounts of resources engaging with Traditional Owner groups, getting them to decide on the process to elect their leaders, getting the groups to give their leaders the authority to sit at the table ... So the media—by interviewing people who were either disgruntled with the process or had alternative agendas or who just had a 'no gas' opinion—created a fake Indigenous position of opposition. And what it really was, is they were individual Indigenous citizens of Australia objecting. The media undermined the integrity of a good process by elevating individual voices, so they were perceived as a collective position.

'What was becoming clear to me was that the mainstream media did not understand how to engage with Indigenous people or how to tell Indigenous stories properly.'

* * *

As the time neared to present the Heads of Agreement to the Goolarabooloo and Jabirr Jabirr claim group, there was still one outstanding principle irking Wayne. The WA Government didn't believe Traditional Owners should be entitled to royalties. Wayne, Cameron Syme and the negotiating team were down in Perth. Wayne recalls meeting Premier Barnett at 7.30 in the evening. He argued convincingly that both the state and Traditional Owners should receive royalty payments, and he recalls the premier finally yielding, 'Okay, okay. Let's do a royalty.' A press release, to be issued the following morning, was prepared by Premier Barnett's office, and Wayne breathed a sigh of relief. He felt he'd had a significant win. He was confident the agreement was now as strong as it could be.

That's when he made a major strategic mistake.

Directly after meeting with the premier, Wayne caught up with some of Woodside's representatives. While he didn't discuss the issue of royalties, they were alarmed the Aboriginal leader had met the premier without them. 'Woodside's warning bells rang through the roof. They wanted to find out what the hell the premier had committed to. The following morning we were summoned to Parliament House. Premier Barnett told us he couldn't sign off on a royalty because Woodside had issues with it. I was disappointed, but as the Heads of Agreement was non-binding, I knew the door was still open for us to negotiate it down the track. The whole incident reinforced to me how close the mining industry was to the government. They were hand in glove.'

With everything finalised, Wayne didn't feel relief—instead, as a thirty-nine-year-old with a young family at home and the future of the Kimberley resting on his shoulders, he felt 'enormous pressure'. He knew Woodside had expectations. And Barnett had expectations. Would these expectations be met? He had no idea. He had no idea whether the Goolarabooloo and Jabirr Jabirr Traditional Owners would vote in support of the agreement. 'I had to remind myself, from KLC's perspective, this was about delivering a process. My job was to put Traditional Owners in the strongest position possible to say either yes or no.'

* * *

On 14 and 15 April, two weeks after Premier Barnett's deadline, Goolarabooloo and Jabirr Jabirr native title claimants made their way to Broome's Mercure Inn Continental. They passed the milky waters of Roebuck Bay and the crab-thick shadows of cabbage palms. They crossed the hotel's car park, where, twenty-one years earlier, two drunk white men laid their beery and blood-rinsed eyes on the KLC chairman's son.

Goolarabooloo and Jabirr Jabirr people filed past the reception into a function room overlooking banana lounges and the chlorine lacquer of the hotel's pool. The room's outlook might have been tranquil, but the energy between the four walls was riven with tension.

Wayne Barker, a Jabirr Jabirr man who went on to spend more than eleven years heading up the Kimberley Aboriginal Law and Culture Centre, was co-chair of the Traditional Owner negotiating committee. During meetings he was carefully expressionless, acquiring a reputation from both the WA Government and Woodside as being a man of stone. But Barker had a gift for reading a room. On the first morning of the Heads of Agreement meeting, he recalls, 'We were all milling around in this nervous kind of space. This was unknown territory for us … Overshadowing the negotiations—though not present—were industry and government. They were in lockstep with each other. They carried their power openly. We felt like we were little fish in a big pond with some big sharks in the water. When people start promising the world, someone's gotta pay for it, and that someone was probably going to be us.'

Frank Parriman, also co-chair of the Traditional Owner negotiating committee, notes that to get to this point there were times when the WA Government and Woodside seemed insincere. 'They could be a bit patronising, a bit disingenuous. They tried to play both sides of the table. *I agree with you*, they'd say. *You guys are doing a great job. I wish we could do more* … All that bullshit came out!'

There were other tensions in the room—emotional, psychological—a blooming understanding that Goolarabooloo had sided with conservationists, whereas Jabirr Jabirr were more inclined to fight for their rights inside the space, within the bounds of native title law.

That morning Barker felt an additional emotional dread, a sense the agreement was a done deal. 'Then I thought—no. This is our country. I realised if we were going to enter into an agreement, then it would be as equals. Because I did not want a gas plant. I absolutely did not want a gas plant.'

Nor did he wish to see the continual suffering of his people.

'Our community is traumatised, ridden with violence, dysfunction and hatred. Somehow, we're trapped. We're trapped in this space. We see the demons, we see the ghosts, we see the shadows, we know they exist, and somehow, we pray they won't consume us.

'When we went to negotiate a better future, it was this that drove me, not the money, not the power. It was to try and unhitch this trauma. Because we don't have a future here, with the rates of suicide and drug abuse. Our community is slowly imploding, deconstructing. The violence is unbelievable. I know Bergmann feels that. We weren't doing this because we wanted a gas plant. We wanted to get off our knees. To create a handhold, or a foothold, to pull ourselves off our knees, to our feet.'

And so the Goolarabooloo and Jabirr Jabirr people found their seats in what Barker recalls was a room of 'smoking grenades'. They turned their eyes to Cameron Syme. Wayne was confident in Syme's ability to present the agreement. 'Cameron was very good; he had a good style. We'd worked together on Tanami Gold, Kimberley Nickel and Koolan Island—three key native title agreements. He spoke in clear, simple English and had a way of framing complex legal terms so everyone in the room could understand. During the meeting, he projected each clause, then talked through it.'

Syme stressed that the Heads of Agreement, should Traditional Owners vote in favour of it, would provide the framework to negotiate the whole suite of Browse Agreements.

Wayne also had a clear message for Traditional Owners, which he'd articulated before. 'My advice was: *If you want to say no, you need to do so now. It's like a funnel. If you slide too far down, it's really hard to climb back out again.* But no-one said no. Everyone was interested to hear the presentation, hear what was on the table, hear the terms of the agreement.'

Later, Justice Wilcox wrote that during the meeting 'People were told the proposal was for a "gas factory, a little thing nobody would see"' (Wilcox). He didn't quote a source nor appear to be aware of the trip Traditional Owners had taken to the Burrup. Both Barker and Wayne dismiss Justice Wilcox's claim as false, insulting to the intelligence of the senior people and Traditional Owners present. Traditional Owners were under no illusions that it was a 'little thing'—neither physically nor spiritually.

What *was* discussed, at length, was the premier's threat of compulsory acquisition: did it still stand? To gain clarity for the group, Wayne excused himself from the meeting and rang Barnett.

'The premier said he would use compulsory acquisition if he needed to. He also said if we signed up, he would take his foot off the accelerator on compulsory acquisition while we negotiated a binding agreement. Considering this, the decision to vote for or against the agreement wasn't "free". The premier was still making the threat. I went back to the claim group and repeated what he'd said.'

If the decision couldn't be made with free, prior and informed consent, should Traditional Owners proceed and vote on the agreement? They decided they should. The group's preferred voting method was a show of hands. But before the agreement could be voted on, the tension Barker had picked up on between the Goolarabooloo and Jabirr Jabirr—a tension over who were the *actual* Traditional Owners for the country in question—at last boiled over. In Joseph Roe's view, the land for James Price Point had been given to him by his grandfather. He had the right to speak for and to make decisions about that land. But not all the Jabirr Jabirr descendants saw it this way—Paddy Roe was Nyikina after all. In Barker's memory, 'Joe was off to one side. We were a unified group. Joe was not. He was a supercharged character and his default was to stand up, bluster, kick over a chair and storm out. He did this at the Heads of Agreement, perhaps thinking if he left the room, negotiations would cease. He assumed we would have to come to him.'

Joe wasn't the only one who walked out.

About a quarter of the attendees at the meeting left with him.

Wayne turned to the remaining Traditional Owners. 'Well, what do we do, guys? It's your call. You're here to make the decision.' The rest of the group decided to proceed, and the resolution—that the claim group authorised the KLC to sign the Heads of Agreement—was put to a vote.

It passed unanimously.

* * *

Should Aboriginal people make decisions by voting? Not according to Greens WA MLC Robin Chapple—a non-Aboriginal man—who told the WA parliament this on two separate occasions: 'The idea of yes or no is a concept that is not embraced by Indigenous communities. For me to say no against somebody who is saying yes is culturally inappropriate' and 'people need to understand how Indigenous people actually conduct their business. Voting is not the norm' (Parliamentary Debates 5314, 'Browse [Land] Agreement Bill' 16).

Wayne took a dim view of this perspective, believing it undermined Traditional Owners' right to choose an appropriate decision-making process, as described under Section 251 of the *Native Title Act 1993*. 'Groups can make a decision in accordance with traditional laws and customs, or as the group decides. In this case, the group decided to vote with a show of hands. It was their decision. Not my decision. Not KLC's decision.'

Justice Wilcox was also critical of the meeting's process. He took issue with the meeting notice (published in the *Broome Advertiser* and in a separate flyer), in which there was no mention a vote would be taken at all. He speculated, 'No doubt for this reason, few G/JJ people attended' (Wilcox).

Wayne was dismissive. 'A former judge applying some kind of standard to a process that was non-binding was a joke—a classic case of backseat commentary from someone on the other side of Australia. There were numerous meetings authorising the negotiations—Joseph Roe was on the committee that negotiated the Heads of Agreement. Any Goolarabooloo or Jabirr Jabirr person sincerely interested in proposed developments on their country made an effort to attend that meeting. Traditional Owners knew they were making a serious decision about their own future.'

Ahead of the launch of his book *Kimberley at the Crossroads*

Wilcox admitted to being unaware that there had even been a Traditional Owner negotiating committee (Hingston and Jones).

Both Wilcox's and Chapple's comments served to harden Wayne's growing disdain for environmentalists. 'The environmental movement was there to support Traditional Owners only if their position was "no". It raised questions about the environmentalists' long-term rank-and-file support of the Indigenous movement. When what we wanted didn't align with "environmental" or "green" values, they undermined our right to self-determination.

'Many cultures have used natural resources, in some way, to improve their lives. Traditionally, we used materials to make tools to maintain a life. We're not frozen in time. It *is* okay for Aboriginal people to think about their natural resources and how they might benefit from using these resources for commercial development. Why shouldn't Aboriginal people be able to negotiate deals with proponents, with mining companies? It's up to individual groups to make their decision about what they do.'

In the wake of the meeting, the situation within the native title claim group became more volatile. Members lost faith in Joseph Roe's leadership and his capacity to represent them. They proceeded with a 66B application under the Native Title Act to have him removed as a named applicant. The group wanted transparency and accountability—a reset to the representation, to ensure applicants took instructions from the whole group. They put their best leadership forward and voted in six new named applicants. Later, Roe challenged the claim group's decision in the Federal Court but was unsuccessful.

For Nolan Hunter, a proud Bardi man who was serving as deputy CEO of the Kimberley Land Council, the biggest issue was anti-gas protesters didn't understand or didn't wish to understand native title processes and KLC's statutory obligations.

'There's proper governance and proper notice under the *Native Title Act 1993*. But the protesters wanted to ignore any process stipulated at law. They blatantly refused to acknowledge that if the claimants were to make any decisions, they needed to do so within accordance of the requirements of the Act. By this refusal, they disrespected native title holders' rights to make fully informed decisions.'

Nolan was two decades into a career that spanned continents—his work in immigration and humanitarian programs, as well as Indigenous affairs, had taken him as far afield as Russia, America and Morocco. On the job, he was admired for his searing intellect; off the job, it was his extraordinary breath-hold while spearfishing, and his night-time crabbing missions past the lairs of saltwater crocodiles which earned him respect.

Nolan was fearless.

He didn't rattle easily.

But the pressure was starting to build.

'What I was really astounded by, what I could not fathom, was how the Aboriginal people running the "no" campaign could be so vicious, venomous, vindictive and malicious, in using Wayne and KLC as scapegoats. In order to tell a good story, you need a good villain.'

In this story, the villain shifted, switched faces, was alternately Wayne or Woodside or Barnett or fly-in-fly-out greenies—it all depended on who was doing the telling.

6: I challenge anyone to take that kind of fire

Off the Tanami Road—a thousand kilometres of gravel potholes connecting Halls Creek with Alice Springs—past the spooky and storied meteorite crater at Wolfe Creek, near an old, rasping windmill, the Bergmann's family treasure was buried.

Ferdy had discovered the treasure by accident in 1964. He was drilling a bore with an old mud puncher he'd found mounted atop a donkey cart years earlier. The donkey's harnesses were stretched out, as if the previous owner had looked around the desert in despair and disgust, unhooked his donkey and walked off toward an easier life. Or maybe the donkey had died.

In any case, Ferdy, searching for water with the old mud puncher, drilled down to five feet, then ten, thirty, a hundred feet. Instead of water, he found an artery of gold, copper and silver. He didn't have the tools to extract the treasure then. So he filled up the hole, covered his tracks and tore loops through the scrub to confuse his companions.

The problem was he confused himself as well.

Decades later he still hadn't been able to locate the site. Wayne had taken out an exploration licence, which overlaid Tanami Downs Stations, so the whole family could continue to scour the area. While family missions had been luckless so far, they weren't willing to give up—not yet. In 2009, just shy of Wayne's fortieth birthday, he set off with his two youngest children, Jarred and Tessa. His younger brother Ferdinand Jnr and Ferdy accompanied them in a separate car. Wayne walked the ridges with his children, keeping an eye out for signs of his dad's old camp and drilling site. 'It was hard country, but extremely beautiful. We walked through mulga trees, bloodwood, spinifex. In the distance were low ranges: black, or dark purple.'

A few days in, on a faint, overgrown track that led to Graveyard Bore, the tyres on the vehicles were 'almost ripped to shreds' by the country's teeth—thorns, stakes, wattle sticks and sharp rocks. The men were constantly repumping and replugging them. Then the compressor broke. Wayne told his dad and brother he'd backtrack toward Tanami Downs homestead, then would continue to Alice Springs to buy a new one. Tessa and Jarred piled into the car with him. Wayne, in a rush to get going, had failed to pack sufficient water—only two litres for the three of them.

* * *

Chris realised something was wrong two days later.

She'd just received a satellite phone call from Ferdinand Jnr.

'Has Wayne called yet?'

'What do you mean?' she asked.

'He was heading to Alice to get a compressor. He left two days ago. He's got the kids.'

Chris willed down a reflux surge of alarm. She promised to call back soon. She went online and checked their shared bank account. There had been no EFTPOS transactions for days. She called the Tanami Downs homestead. The managers hadn't seen Wayne or the children. She called Rabbit Flat Roadhouse, where the family would've—should've—filled up. There'd been no sign of Wayne there either.

'That's when I started panicking. I rang Ferdinand back and begged him to start looking for them.'

* * *

Wayne was crawling along in low-range four-wheel drive when he felt one of the tyres blow. He slowed. A mistake. Two more tyres blew. Wayne killed the engine. They were out of spares. Had no compressor.

He took stock of the situation.

On the upside, they had a GPS, sleeping bags and snacks.

On the downside, they only had two litres of water. They were unlikely to be rescued by any station people, given they'd just made their own track, and Ferdinand Jnr and Ferdy wouldn't come looking—they'd think Wayne could handle himself.

Wayne could handle himself, he was comfortable in the bush. But he was worried about his children.

Jarred was only ten and Tessa was seven.

With so little water, he knew if they stayed with the car that by the time someone came looking they'd find three dead bodies. There was a windmill and water fifteen kilometres to the north as the crow flies. The station's homestead was about forty kilometres to the north-east. It made sense to strike out to the windmill. Wayne told the children to grab what they could carry. Tessa put on her pink pyjamas, thongs, and grabbed her pillow.

The pillow and pyjamas were good choices. Wayne ended up borrowing the pillow for himself that evening, and the pyjamas stopped the spinifex from completely lacerating Tessa's legs. By evening they still hadn't reached the windmill. They pulled up on a gust-scalloped sandhill. The night was drawing in cold—below ten degrees. Wayne remembered stories from the old desert people he'd worked with in Fitzroy, remembered how they would dig sand cocoons, build a fire within the cocoon, then cover the coals with a cooler layer of sand on which to sleep. He did this for the kids and tucked them into their sleeping bags. They were soon dreaming.

But Wayne couldn't sleep.

He watched over the sleeping bodies of his children with a heightened feeling of anxiety.

He thought about what one old desert woman had told him, how, during one terrible drought a long, long time ago, many children had died. The jilas, the permanent waterholes, had almost been dry. There wasn't enough water to go around.

Wayne had been careful through the day, only giving the children tiny sips. But what would happen if one of the kids got heat stroke? He could carry Tessa on his shoulders. She'd already developed a blister on one of her feet which had swelled to the size of a fist, and he'd had to carry her for most of the afternoon. But if it were Jarred … well, Jarred was too big. He wouldn't be able to carry him.

A hundred kilometres distant he could hear the soughing of trucks on the Tanami Road. He could see their lights in the sky. Sound and light travel a long way in the desert at night. And yet here, they were completely alone.

That evening he realised how at risk they were.

* * *

They got to the windmill at around ten the next morning and each had a long, cool drink. Once Wayne had refilled the water bottle, he looked around. There was some old plastic and PVC piping. He built a fire then fed the garbage into it, hoping the grubby smoke might catch someone's attention.

'But we were in the middle of nowhere. No-one saw it. There was an old grader, or tractor, so we tried to get that going, but the battery was flat. Then we realised one of the sleeping bags had fallen out of the backpack along the way. That's when I knew we had to start walking again.'

Wayne ripped some fabric from his shirt to make bandages for Tessa's foot, then he lifted her onto his shoulders. At least from here they were on an actual station road and had a better chance of being picked up. Tessa and Jarred were quiet, uncomplaining. They walked for another hour. The sun was straightening toward its scorching zenith. In the distance they saw some cars. They waved their arms, shouted. The cars didn't slow. They kept walking, pausing every so often in the shade for a sip of water.

In the forefront of his mind, Wayne was focused on survival, on getting the children home safe. But his subconscious mind was also churning with work stresses. He was due in Canberra in a couple of days for a meeting with federal government ministers to discuss the social impacts of a gas plant. A lot rested on this meeting. Traditional Owners were relying on him.

Late in the afternoon Wayne heard the rumble of a vehicle behind them. It was a Toyota, from the station. It slowed and Wayne nearly wept with relief.

The family climbed up into the back of the ute tray.

'I'll never forget the feeling of being on the back of that Toyota, with the wind blowing through our hair. We were safe.'

At the homestead, the managers were an Aboriginal couple—the woman's dad knew and had worked with Ferdy. They prepared a rich and fragrant beef stew with rice for the family. It was their first meal in two days. Wayne and Tessa tucked in, starving. Jarred declined. He'd been diagnosed with autism a couple of years earlier and had always been sensitive about his food—even now, with an achingly empty belly.

Chris thinks this was a pivotal moment for Wayne in recognising and accepting his son's autism. 'Often dads initially struggle with this acceptance. When it came to Jarred's sensitivity around food, I think Wayne thought I was being too soft on him, pandering to him. But Jarred still had his food sensitivities, even after not eating for two days. The couple ended up giving him some white bread and butter.'

On top of this, Wayne was battling guilt. He felt he'd come dangerously close to being responsible for his children's deaths.

He didn't have a chance to properly process the ordeal.

Over the next few days he flew with the children on a charter flight to Darwin, then took the red-eye from Darwin to Canberra. Wayne had gone from nearly dying in the desert to wearing a suit and greeting three of the most influential ministers in the country.

The meeting was a disaster.

* * *

With negotiations for a final Indigenous Land Use Agreement (ILUA) between Woodside, the WA Government and Traditional Owners still underway, a sticking point which Wayne felt hadn't been addressed by either the state or federal governments was the social impact. Both governments would gain from Woodside's project through royalties—but at what cost to the local Aboriginal community? How could each government mitigate potential impacts? Wayne had spearheaded an Aboriginal social impact assessment process involving consultations with more than eighty-eight Indigenous organisations which would be affected by the development. KLC visited communities from Bidyadanga to Ardyaloon, and Traditional Owner concerns were compiled in a report designed to assist the federal government in prioritising funding down the track. At this meeting he also wanted to discuss the Commonwealth's potential contribution to a regional benefits fund.

Wayne cordially greeted the attorney-general, the federal resources minister and Indigenous affairs minister Jenny Macklin.

But after two sleepless nights his patience was in short supply.

'The Commonwealth talks a particular bureaucratic language. I've never been comfortable with it. I'm a direct shooter, I'm straight down the line. They were giving me these roundabout answers, talking in riddles. I had no idea whether they were going to make a commitment or not. I'd had enough!'

Wayne had slept very little for several days. He had post-traumatic stress. He went on the attack, demanding answers of the minister for Indigenous affairs, turning up the heat.

Jenny Macklin's voice began to crack.

Wayne didn't let up on her, didn't realise it was time to stop.

The minister burst into tears.

One of the attorney-general's senior advisors contacted Cameron Syme after the meeting. 'In all my years as an advisor,' he said, 'that was the worst meeting I have ever attended.'

While this particular meeting didn't stand out to Ciaran O'Faircheallaigh, he recalls the Commonwealth's lack of commitment was a great source of disappointment. 'The Commonwealth refused to contribute. They were going to get, by far, the lion's loot from the precinct through corporate taxes, because most of the project was offshore. But they just weren't coming to the party.'

Chris remembers when Wayne got home from Canberra, he was shattered. She'd already pulled the pin on his fortieth birthday celebrations.

'People thought Wayne was a man of the mining companies. They didn't see he was fighting them all day. They had no idea what went on behind closed doors. Wayne was fighting Woodside, the federal government, the state government. He wasn't able to reveal that he'd been fighting them. He had to step out of those meetings and pretend everything was okay. And they could hide behind Wayne, in a way. He was up the front, in the public eye, copping it all.'

Wayne, too, was starting to feel the temperature rise. 'I got the sense people were really angry. KLC wasn't keeping the community informed. But we weren't resourced to do that. And because of the confidentiality agreements, we couldn't reveal everything that was going on. Our job was to represent Traditional Owners and not the broader non-Indigenous community.'

* * *

In August 2009, a well-head blew at the Montara offshore oil rig operated by PTTEP Australasia. Each day, for seventy-five days, hundreds of barrels of oil were discharged into the ocean, strangling sea snakes and gluing the feathers of brown boobies. On the water, fishermen observed a dark sheen that came within twenty kilometres of the Kimberley coast. In eastern Indonesia, seaweed farmers lost their livelihoods. Their skin lifted in pus-tight cysts and darkened with strange bruises. The Labor-led Australian Government ignored their calls for compensation.

It was one of Australia's worst oil disasters.

It went almost unreported.

But conservationists were paying attention, calling for a toughening of regulations to prevent similar incidents. Should a comparable spill occur in the Browse Basin, there were fears the oil would swathe the length of the Dampier Peninsula in a single tide cycle.

* * *

Despite the lengthy work behind the scenes by Woodside and Traditional Owners, the federal and state governments were becoming irritated by the glacial pace at which the project was progressing. Woodside's joint venture partners hadn't committed to a development plan at James Price Point and hadn't made a final investment decision. They were still courting two options preferred by some protesters: piping the gas to the Pilbara or processing it for export on floating platforms. At the end of 2009, the WA Government issued an ultimatum—the joint venture partners must agree to an LNG hub at James Price Point within 120 days. If they didn't, they'd risk losing their retention leases.

It also put the heat on Traditional Owners. In-fighting between the Goolarabooloo and Jabirr Jabirr had seen the final agreement deadline extended three times. Finally, sick of the indecision, Premier Barnett did what he'd been threatening to do from the get-go—he pulled the trigger on compulsory acquisition.

Wayne recalls the premier telling him in person. 'Barnett

was very nice. His voice was very nice. Then, all of a sudden, his tone changed. It was like flicking a switch. He was about to be a commander. *Sorry, Wayne, I have no choice. I have to give industry certainty.* I felt deflated. I had doubts over James Price Point as a good location. The Anjo Peninsula, from a technical perspective, was the best location, and the Wunambal Gaambera people had given their written consent. I told the premier, *The wheels are going to fall off. The capacity for Traditional Owners to make a decision has been railroaded.*'

Premier Barnett's announcement that the government would seize the land through compulsory acquisition was cautiously welcomed by Woodside and condemned by conservation groups. Save The Kimberley's chairperson, Peter Tucker, called the Broome community to action, saying it was 'gloves off now' (Prior 'Outrage' 1).

Almost one thousand people marched in protest from Broome's Male Oval to Town Beach. A flotilla of kayaks circled one of Woodside's jackup rigs three kilometres offshore from James Price Point. Conservation groups bombed the premier's affluent home electorate of Cottesloe with eighteen thousand leaflets reading *The Kimberley: Like Nowhere Else on Earth*. And a man set off to see the prime minister in Canberra, leading a camel laden with twelve thousand postcards of protest.

Green heavyweights were also ready to brawl. Senator Bob Brown swept into the Kimberley, asking Woodside and Shell why none of the alternatives to an onshore gas plant were okay. Geoff Cousins, a corporate maverick famous for taking on timber giant Gunns in Tasmania, muscled his way into the debate, writing, 'A social licence to operate is what is required, not just some backroom deal' (Cousins 14). Missy Higgins had been joined by fellow musician Rob Hirst from Midnight Oil, as well as Xavier Rudd and John Butler—Butler donated part of his ticket sales to Save The Kimberley and Joseph Roe to help bankroll Roe's ongoing legal actions against KLC and the WA Government.

For protesters, this publicity was a boon. It drew national attention. It meant Woodside and the state government couldn't ignore the people of Broome opposed to the gas plant. Their ranks were swelling. They wouldn't be duped into thinking the plant would be 'a very big fridge sitting on the beach', as Woodside might like them to believe (McGeough 65).

With the escalation of the issue, a menacing side of the protest movement revealed itself.

For Chris and the children, living in Broome was becoming intolerable.

* * *

It started with little things. When Chris was out and about, friends would cross to the other side of the road, heads down, to avoid speaking with her. At school sports day, the parents of other children would turn their backs when she approached. *Oh my God*, Chris remembers thinking. *They hate me*. Chris and Wayne's children walked to school along pavements bright with anti-gas graffiti about their dad. Teachers were openly opposed to the gas plant on the radio. One teacher invited Wayne into his class to give a presentation about KLC's process to counterbalance a talk by a conservation group. There was savage backlash from some of the parents.

'Up until that point, Wayne had been the hero, the environmental warrior, the land rights champion. We felt like we belonged. Now, we were on the side that nobody loved. We stopped going out and really cut back on socialising for fear of being attacked. I was always anxious about who might be there. I set up a fake account on Facebook so I could see who was talking behind our backs. I realised we had so few friends left. Apart from very close family, and one or two friends, we were completely isolated.'

Nolan Hunter recalls Wayne being criticised with venom and malice in heated verbal exchanges and in written condemnations in the local newspaper and online. One post, playing on Wayne's last name, depicted him as a 'Burger Man': in the middle of a hamburger, being fucked by Woodside on one side and the state government on the other. Nolan says, 'To think that somebody in Broome could post this... Through his career Wayne had been selfless. He'd built his career on sacrifice and dedication to Traditional Owners. Then to turn around and cop this! I challenge anyone to try and stand in Wayne's shoes and take that kind of fire.'

Fire came, too, in the form of strange clicks and static which interrupted the family's conversations on their home phone. Wayne and Chris suspected their phone was being tapped.

Fire came in the form of death threats.

After school one day, Sara found her dad sitting at the family's computer in the living room. 'Come and have a look at this,' he said, grinning. Sara looked over his shoulder. A stranger had sent Wayne a personal Facebook message threatening to kill him. Her heart began to race. 'They must think I'm so important,' Wayne laughed.

Sara took several deep breaths. If her dad wasn't afraid, then she shouldn't be afraid either.

Still, it was impossible for her to pretend there was nothing going on.

She'd recently been accosted by a girl she went to school with, a girl she'd known for years. 'This girl was in my ear, *So, are you for, or against, the gas?*'

Sara shrugged. 'Why would that involve me? I'm not for or against. I think I'm neutral.'

The girl's aggression prompted Sara to share the encounter with her parents. 'Give her my phone number,' Wayne said.

The next day at school Sara handed the girl a slip of paper. 'Dad says if you have a problem, you can call him.'

Wayne preferred to be on the front foot ahead of attacks. In Sara's memory, 'If Dad was at the Boulevard and saw someone who'd been bad mouthing him—having no sense of social cues—he'd go up them and say, *How's it going? What have you been up to? I hear you've been saying stuff about me?*[12] There was no sense Dad was intimidated.'

Wayne and Chris had never wanted to send their children to boarding school in Perth, but they were worried things might get worse, especially for Sara. They encouraged her to apply for a Year 10 scholarship at Presbyterian Ladies' College.

She was successful.

She was also distraught.

Boarding in Perth would mean being separated from her younger brother, Jarred.

Sara had learned about Jarred's autism when she was in Year 7 —Tessa's diagnosis came three years later. 'We had our first ever family meeting. It was really formal and really uncomfortable. Jarred was running around, being his weird and wonderful self, saying having autism made him superhuman and superior to everyone else … I had to process the guilt I had about being so mean to him. I didn't realise he'd had no control over the things that annoyed me.'

Year 10 for Sara coincided with Jarred's first year at high school in Broome. It was this that upset her the most.

'How was I supposed to protect him, to watch out for him?

How was he going to understand all the social cues? I wasn't even thinking about James Price Point. I couldn't understand why they would send me away when my brother needed me.'

By this stage, Chris was crying every day.

'I felt so bitter. We had given up so much of our lives for Wayne to fight this fight. And then the state would stab him. And Woodside would stab him. And the Traditional Owners would stab him. And friends and colleagues and family would stab him—with no respect for what he had given up to do this job.'

Wayne says. 'I'd become a dictator. That was the criticism. I was a dictator, and if it wasn't Wayne's way, it was the highway. I didn't see myself as a dictator. I saw myself as putting Traditional Owners in the strongest possible position to make decisions.'

He was nearing burnout.

'I needed another challenge. I was tired of talking about the same stuff. A year in a land council is like working ten years in private practice. I remember saying to Ciaran, *What is it about all these non-believers, these nutters, always attacking me?* And Ciaran said, *Only a handful of land councils around Australia get attacked. And the reason is because they are the ones pushing the envelope. Making a change. Making a difference.*'

* * *

The final suite of Browse Agreements, soon to be presented to the Goolarabooloo and Jabirr Jabirr native title groups, had the potential to make a profound difference. Enshrined in the agreements was a commitment to help Traditional Owners generate wealth through business and employment opportunities, a housing fund encouraging home ownership, an education fund to increase the number of Kimberley Aboriginal students finishing Year 12 and continuing further study, and a cultural preservation fund targeted at young people at risk. The WA Government would agree to grant Traditional Owners six hundred hectares of freehold (or other) land and commit to paying fifteen million dollars for the creation of conservation and heritage areas. It would also maintain an environmental compliance officer at the hub for the whole of its life. In Ciaran O'Faircheallaigh's view, 'One of the fundamental problems is that governments don't police environmental laws. So, getting an officer for the whole life of a project, and having control over a fundamental design aspect of a project, was remarkable.' Traditional Owners would be paid some of the money upfront, regardless of whether the project went ahead. The Browse LNG Precinct Regional Benefits Agreement would deal with the ripple effects of development across the whole Kimberley.

The agreements—worth 1.5 billion dollars for Traditional Owners—set a new precedent and would come to represent the high watermark of Indigenous agreement-making across Australia. It was a stark contrast to the agreements negotiated relating to four LNG processing plants on Curtis Island, near Gladstone in Central Queensland. The plants were expected to process twice as much LNG as the Browse precinct, cost twice as much to build, and yet, according to Traditional Owners, the agreements were likely worth less than ten million dollars. Wayne reflects, 'Our process was of such high integrity, such quality. When people don't have proper legal representation, or the backing of a highly political land council, they get poor outcomes.'

To further support Traditional Owners' right to self-determination, Wayne had lobbied the federal government to grant the West Kimberley a place on the national heritage list. With heritage listing confirmed in August 2011, an extra layer of heritage protection meant mining companies had to contend with a more rigorous approvals process. He'd also done something no other Traditional Owner group had attempted in the history of the state. Drawing upon all his legal knowledge and the A-team of lawyers in his orbit, Wayne successfully convinced the WA Government to pass a law which meant James Price Point was the *only* site gas could be processed on the whole Kimberley coast. Wayne was honouring the commitment he'd articulated in the joint position statement with the conservation groups back in 2007. According to Premier Barnett, it was 'the first time in this State's history that Parliament had been asked to ratify an agreement reached between the State and indigenous West Australians' ('LNG Precinct'). The *Browse (Land) Agreement Act 2012* provided for the rehabilitation of the land after the gas precinct life and ensured the land would be returned to Traditional Owners. The new law couldn't be changed unless consent was given by both houses of parliament and by the Traditional Owners.

Wayne achieved these outcomes despite a suite of a deeply racist beliefs held by non-Aboriginal people weighing into the debate. There was a popular and pervasive view that Kimberley Aboriginal leaders who had attended university were less connected to their country and culture. In a letter to the editor published by the *Broome Advertiser* in April 2011, Wayne was accused of being so far removed from tradition and culture that he was willing to sell his soul and the land to the devil for a buck. In *Heritage Fight*, a film about the protests, a non-Aboriginal woman who no longer lives in Broome addressed the camera, 'We've got Indigenous people getting a kartiya education, having no connection to country or law, and coming back to their people with the pure notion of cashing in on their ignorance. So, you've got people like myself, who are kartiya, who fight tooth and nail for culture and country, then you've got also Indigenous people who are fighting tooth and nail to sell it' (Dumont 18:22–18:43). Save The Kimberley issued a report in which the author, Peter Botsman, a writer and scholar based in NSW, puts forth the view, 'Certainly modern meetings in motels with PowerPoint presentations might well look comprehensive, votes around board tables or in bough shades might seem fair but if they do not take into account the rigours and requirements of customary law they will invariably fail to be respected by Indigenous people. This is compounded by the tendency for leaders who have mastered European education and communications to have a louder voice on these matters than those who are well versed in traditional law and culture' (Botsman 43).

The intimation—that perhaps Wayne and other KLC leaders were in a position to hoodwink or bully their countrymen on account of a university education—reflects a deep ignorance of Kimberley leadership structures. Wayne would not have been appointed chief executive of the land council had he not had the cultural support from the Traditional Owners who schooled him up during his KALACC days. These same Traditional Owners, aware of how their people had been run over roughshod by governments and companies in the past, encouraged Wayne to attain a Bachelor of Laws so he could fight for Traditional Owner rights within a white system.

The way Nyikina and Jabirr Jabirr man Anthony Watson saw it, 'We were fighting with people who never wanted to give Traditional Owners the right to make a decision. We were called cavemen. We were expected to be cavemen or bushmen—not to be political. They were offensive words.'

When it came to the often-repeated suggestion that the consultation process was not culturally sound, Nolan Hunter says, 'Nobody wanted to find out the facts. They did not respect that Wayne had ensured strong cultural governance was in place, or that the process was guided by senior cultural leadership.'

Wayne was sick of being judged by outsiders and appalled at the whispers he was on the take and would stand to personally benefit from the Browse Agreements. He wouldn't. He was paid a wage by KLC—that was it. He was also sick of managing the storm of misinformation surrounding the project. 'The pressure that we felt … we never had the resources to push back on the propaganda. As an activist strategy, it's a great strategy, that's what their job was to do, to create uncertainty. But for us, for me, it was exhausting.'

Wayne announced his retirement from the land council in March 2011. Although he was stepping away, he would continue as chief negotiator for the James Price Point proposal. It was almost time to present the final Browse LNG Precinct Project Agreement to the entire Goolarabooloo and Jabirr Jabirr claim group. A month prior to the vote, Wayne ensured every family group was given a private presentation on the details of the agreement so they could understand the legalese and make an informed decision about whether or not they wished to support it.

* * *

The agreement was signed through a backdoor deal! They only had people who voted yes there; they even flew people in who they knew would vote yes! It wasn't a secret vote, like it should have been! There were children voting! Bergmann threatened Traditional Owners. He said, If you don't vote, it will go ahead anyway!

These were the wildfire rumours burning in the wake of the final native title meeting on 6 May, during which Goolarabooloo and Jabirr Jabirr people were given the opportunity to vote in favour or against the agreement.

The meeting was held at the Broome Convention Centre. It was conducted through a legally sound process run independent of the KLC through the National Native Title Tribunal. There were voting officials and scrutineers. Traditional Owners voted by secret ballot.

Frank Parriman, co-chair of the Traditional Owner negotiating committee, recalls the tone of the meeting was 'sombre on both sides'. As with many Traditional Owners, the negotiations had wreaked havoc on his personal life. 'My family was copping it. My wife was abused three times by white people. Some of my friends objected. Some stopped talking to us and defriended us. But I saw that everyone had a legitimate argument. If people opposed the gas, that was their right. They had a right to do that. They had a perfect right to oppose it, as long as they did it properly …'

To get to this point, Frank says three things happened. 'One, was to get the deal on the table. Two, was about setting a precedent, about saying, *You're not going to get it easy, you're going to have to earn your way.* The third was about establishing the benchmark …'

Ciaran O'Faircheallaigh observed the agreements indeed set a precedent, considering the scale of the benefits and the influence it gave people—nothing as strong had ever been negotiated before and was unlikely to be negotiated after. 'Traditional Owners designed the process, and the government backed the process. Usually someone else has picked the location, someone else has designed the process, then you're reacting to it.'

Wayne looked around the room. While it wasn't the entire Goolarabooloo Jabirr Jabirr claim group, nowhere in the Kimberley had he seen such a huge percentage of a claim group's members in attendance at a native title meeting. Likewise, in a federal election, even under the threat of a fine, there had never been a one hundred percent turnout.

A secret ballot was cast. The votes were counted. One hundred and sixty-four people voted in favour of the agreement and one hundred and eight voted against. Five people abstained.[13]

There were still question marks over the project.

Woodside and its joint venture partners were yet to make a final investment decision.

And final Traditional Owner consent was conditional on the minister for sustainability, environment, heritage and water, Tony Burke, putting in place plans to manage cultural, social and environmental impacts.

These question marks gave conservation groups and protesters hope.

There was still an opportunity to boot Woodside out of the Kimberley.

* * *

A couple of days after the agreement was signed, Wayne, his family and Ciaran flew to Canada, on the back of an offer from senior Cree leaders to visit their country. The leaders, including the deputy grand chief of the Cree Nation, had visited the Kimberley when Traditional Owners were negotiating the principle of a regional benefits sharing agreement. Out of cultural respect the leaders told Wayne if he was ever in Canada, it would be a privilege to show him around.

'We did a seven-day canoe trip along a traditional beaver hunting route. We portaged around waterfalls, collected wild berries, ate geese and ate fish. We camped at the edge of cold lakes. Each night, I was absolutely aching in pain!' It was a welcome change from the intense intellectual work that had occupied the preceding months.

The trip reignited conversations between the Nyikina leader and the Cree about regional benefits sharing. 'In Australia, the concept of regional benefits is not new, with various forms enshrined in the Northern Territory Aboriginal Land Rights Act and by the NSW Land Council in aspects of its work. But I was criticised about this principle by ex-judges, environmental groups and Traditional Owners, when in fact it's a very Traditional Owner principle. It's about looking after people and sharing and it happens every day: in traditional law and custom, in initiation ceremonies, at funerals, when you have a cultural obligation to share. The Cree Nation had decided this principle should form a part of its own agreement-making. So, in terms of royalty payments, half would go to the immediate Traditional Owners and community and the other half would go to the Grand Council of the Crees to support all Cree people.'

The trip provided a brief reprieve.

Wayne was reminded of the strength of Aboriginal culture, globally.

* * *

Back in the Kimberley a convoy of vehicles was travelling to Woodside's worksite. It was 7 June 2011. The company had begun work clearing vegetation and investigating whether the soil and water would be suitable for their project. But at a red bottleneck of road near James Price Point, it ground to a halt. A car had been wrecked sideways, blocking traffic in either direction. Within moments the convoy was surrounded by more than a dozen protesters, including Joseph Roe, Greens WA MLC Robin Chapple, and a man who slipped from the shrub and locked himself to one of the company's bulldozers. Woodside was forced to turn back to Broome. A week later there was a permanent blockade at the Manari Road turnoff and the number of protesters had swelled to seventy, including musician John Butler, who'd flown his young family north to join the fray.

The gas debate was putting strains on family relationships and old friendships. Maree Gaffney, who'd worked with Chris at Karrayili and played the love songs at the couple's wedding, questioned the Kimberley Land Council's position. She asked Wayne, 'Are you really doing the right thing? Look what's happening to our community!'

There had been a surge of unrest among some of Broome's old Aboriginal families who were aggrieved by the lack of consultation. Shouldn't Woodside or the WA Government have asked them whether they wanted a gas plant? A petition protesting the development was circulated and signed by over two thousand people before it was delivered to the environment minister, Tony Burke. A giant concert was thrown at Cable Beach—the federal government had promised to listen to anti-gas hub concerns if a sufficient number of people attended—and in one estimate there were over seven and a half thousand concertgoers who spilled onto the sand and into the water, listening to bands perform from the deck of a catamaran moored just offshore. Organisers sidestepped shire regulations, describing the event as a 'picnic' for which permits were unnecessary. Permits also weren't required for bands to play on private catamarans. Among the musicians were Broome's Pigram Brothers, who'd wooed the guests at Wayne and Chris's wedding over two decades before.

The event was a sign of community, of solidarity, and for those protesting a gas hub at James Price Point, it was a sign of hope. Hope was in short supply—especially after what had happened a fortnight earlier, on what became known as Black Tuesday.

* * *

For almost a month, the blockade on Manari Road prevented Woodside from accessing its worksite. A major confrontation was brewing. It came on Tuesday 5 July during NAIDOC Week. That morning, a group of old people blocked the road with their camp chairs. They wore hoodies and beanies, propped anti-gas placards against their knees, and crooned songs in the blue pre-dawn.

Their songs would soon become screams.

A pack of one hundred riot police were deployed north from Perth. Together with local police, and trailed by Woodside's convoy, the police fronted up to the blockade where they were greeted with cries of 'Shame' and 'Arrest Barnett'. Sirens wailed. Old people sobbed. A wooden cross bore the wound-red words *Barnett crucifying the Kimberley*.

Then, 'after hours of cat-and-mouse tactics', the police thrust through the blockade, knocking protesters to the ground (Parker). One protester told an officer he knew where all of Broome's police lived. He said he'd go to their homes and kill their families. Another protester, Goolarabooloo woman Janet Cox, later told the court she was frightened when she learned Woodside was bringing in its machines to clear country. She said she was frightened for her children and her grandchildren. She said her skin was the only thing holding her from falling apart. Others weren't frightened, but they believed the premier was using riot police as private security for an oil and gas company. Twenty-five people were arrested.

Black Tuesday marked the day the rift in Broome's community—between those in favour of a gas plant and those in opposition—was at its most stark. It also marked an escalation of racism against the Traditional Owners who had been negotiating for the development of the plant. What Wayne couldn't understand was how this passionate depth of feeling for the Kimberley—for its dugongs and whales and bilbies—didn't also translate to compassion for its people, its children or its children's future.

* * *

In the next month, three young people killed themselves on three consecutive Saturday nights in Wayne's hometown of Derby. Though it was only August, the town's suicide tally for the year had already reached six. The chief executive of Ngunga Women's Resource Centre told *The West* the deaths could be attributed to limited employment options, the extortionate cost of living and the complete absence of hope (Prior, 'In Derby').

Further down the highway, in the remote Kimberley town of Balgo, there had also been a disproportionate number of deaths among young people, including from suicide and petrol sniffing. In the case of the petrol sniffer, when nurses asked what they could do to help the struggling eighteen-year-old, an Aboriginal community health services chairperson suggested they build a coffin. Some young men in the community were even using cockroach bombs to get high.

Wayne was incensed that protesters claimed they loved the Kimberley but were silent on the unfolding human rights crisis around them. 'These suicides never made any major headlines. None of the greenies stood up and said, *This is wrong.* They took a very western view, decolonising country of people.'

Wayne and Chris's old friend, Maree Gaffney, reflects that through James Price Point, 'Wayne saw the opportunity to improve the lot of Aboriginal people. This was at the core of everything he did. Aboriginal people were living in poverty. I wasn't living in poverty, so it was easy for me to sit back and have an opinion.'

Plenty of people in Broome and around Australia had an opinion.

And the most hurtful, the most pernicious opinions, were often anonymous.

* * *

On the outside of the KLC office someone spray-painted: *Killing Land and Culture.* An anti-gas poster in town read: *Who's looking after country? Not you, you black cunts.* Then an anonymous and vile ten-page newsletter began circulating. The newsletter's author accused a number of prominent Kimberley Aboriginal people, including Wayne, Carol Martin, Irene Davey and Anthony Watson of being 'toxic coconuts'. Further text read, 'You think white. You lie white. You talk white. You act white...When the wind blows you can hear the whitemans [sic] money rattling in your pockets.' There was a photo of Nolan Hunter with the words 'Chief Coconut' and 'WOODSIDE S MAGIC: BUSY BLACKS...... TURNS THEM INTO COCONUTS . WOODSIDE EXPLOITING ABORIGINAL GREED .... ARENT YOU WOODSIDE??' [sic]

Conservation groups were quick to distance themselves from the newsletter.

Businessman Geoffrey Cousins rebuked *The Australian* for giving credence to an anonymous source.

A woman wrote to the *Broome Advertiser*, complaining the newsletter cast a slur on *all* those who opposed the gas hub.

For Traditional Owners working for the KLC, the newsletter wasn't an anomaly. Nolan Hunter, KLC's new chief executive, was under constant attack. People screamed 'traitor' as he walked down the streets of Broome. He received a death threat. 'I was really disappointed. I was angry. Here's what exacerbated it—there was a lot of misinformation out there. People were spreading stories, rumours, lies, and nobody wanted to understand Traditional Owner's legal rights to make decisions under native title law about their country. The Kimberley Land Council's statutory function as a native title representative body was to facilitate a process and follow procedures in accordance with native title law to allow Traditional Owners to make those decisions. It was never the role of KLC to make any decisions about Traditional Owners' native title areas on accepting the gas project ... People chose to believe what they wanted to believe, and they did so without talking to Wayne or the KLC to find out the true facts. They were so intent on making Wayne and the KLC the villain that they disregarded and disrespected the senior leaders and cultural bosses who tried to give support to the Traditional Owners of native title who spoke for James Price Point, and to exercise their right under the United Nation's Free, Prior and Informed Consent.'

Irene Davey, one of KLC's cultural advisors, also received a death threat in the mail at One Arm Point. 'I looked at it but I knew I hadn't done anything wrong. I knew there were people on both sides of the story, hoping for the best way to move forward.'

For Jabirr Jabirr man Wayne Barker, the attacks weren't just psychological, but physical. 'On the Day of Souls, I pulled up at the Broome Cemetery. I'd just stopped the car and was getting myself organised when three young fellas ran up. I got king hit—they split my lip, cut my tongue, then ran off.' Barker knew he'd been attacked for co-chairing the Traditional Owner negotiating committee. It was at that moment he understood the image Broome liked to flaunt—that of an integrated and harmonious community—was utterly false.

***

There were ongoing clashes along the Manari Road between protesters and authorities. Two local Broome grandmothers blocked the road with their van and locked it in place with star pickets and drums of quick-drying concrete. A group snuck in to one of Woodside's work camps and quietly unzipped the contractors' mozzie domes. The contractors jolted awake to find themselves face to face with camels—giant teeth glinting wet in the starlight.

Not all protests were so benign.

There's footage of a Woodside convoy transporting Traditional Owners employed by the company to their worksite. An Aboriginal man en route to undertake heritage work sits in the back of a four-wheel drive. The camera pans to a very young white woman. She's screaming at the Aboriginal man through the glass. 'This is what you should be protecting because this is what your grandparents fucking taught you. What did they teach you? Did you go through Law? (Dumont 01:26:29—01:27:06).

The man covers his face with his hands.

Carol Martin knew there were other videos, too, captured by Woodside's Hostile Environment Services. The footage contained images of assault—images of protesters spitting at Traditional Owners. 'I blame Woodside for not getting the information out to the community so they can all see who they are standing next to on that protest line' (I'm No Coconut' 1). It was this footage Wayne lost his temper over. He, too, implored the company to publicise what they'd recorded. 'You need to tell the truth about who these people are,' he told Woodside staff at a meeting in Broome.

Jen Allen, Wayne's executive assistant through the gas days, recalls sitting outside Wayne's office while the meeting took place.

The office was glassed in.

The staff had eyes on their computers and ears cocked to the door. Jen heard Wayne begin to shout. 'Everyone in the office went dead silent. I heard him shout something about his kids getting bullied at school because of this. I could feel and sense the emotion, especially the way his body was moving. And then the tears! *Oh my god*, I thought, *This is huge*. In meetings with mining companies he always had it so together. It was horrendous to see him crack like that. He pushed open the door of the office, sobbing. I was shocked. Horrified. I rang Chris. She was straight on the ball. *I'll go get him, Jen, I'll go meet him. Where's he gone?*'

Wayne had buckled.

Was broken.

It was time to leave Broome.

* * *

In August 2011 Wayne and Chris packed the car for Jarlmadangah, a Nyikina community not far from the river and surrounded by a natural amphitheatre of red cliffs. They borrowed a trailer, hitched it up to the car and packed everything they'd need—a fridge, barbeque, clothes, swags—everything except their dog, Harni, who they left with Wayne's mum in Derby. They were worried the tougher community dogs might kill her. Heartbroken, Harni ran away from Pat Bergmann's home and eventually ended up at Jarlmadangah with the family. The family lived in a caravan for the next six months. Chris volunteered as a literacy teacher at the community school Jarred and Tessa attended. On weekends, desperate to make up for lost time, Wayne shared with them a taste of the life he'd enjoyed growing up with his Nana Aggie. Together they went fishing, hunting, croc-catching and searching for cherrabun.

Within the community, Wayne felt as though he had the support of his wider family, including Anthony Watson, John and Harry Watson and Joe Brown. For Chris, it was the refreshing change the family needed.

'At Jarlmadangah we were able to regroup, get back into a better mental health state. People hadn't heard about James Price Point and the gas. The community was very welcoming—the kids fitted into the school. We felt like we belonged somewhere again.'

* * *

The James Price Point saga wasn't over, but with negotiations finalised months earlier and the agreements formally signed by Goolarabooloo and Jabirr Jabirr in June, Wayne's involvement had lessened.

Over the following two years, board members of the state's Environmental Protection Authority (EPA), responsible for determining environmental approval for the project, were found to have participated in the assessment process, despite extraordinary conflicts of interest. Two members had shares in Woodside and a third worked for BP, one of Woodside's joint venture partners.

Meanwhile, the WA Government—after two bungled attempts at compulsory acquisition—was successful in having native title extinguished over the area. But the process had been a waste of time. Woodside, now with a new CEO, decided development at James Price Point didn't stack up financially. It would reconvene with its joint venture partners to further evaluate floating technologies and a pipeline to existing LNG facilities in the Pilbara.

Sara called Wayne from Perth when she heard Woodside was pulling out. 'That was eight years of my life I didn't have you,' she said to her dad. 'It was all for nothing.'

The federal government was off the hook. It no longer needed to make a politically explosive decision. Conservation groups celebrated Woodside's withdrawal, attributing it to the cohesive and sustained protest movement. They saw it as a remarkable win for the environment: a small community had triumphed over a state government hell-bent on development, and a conglomerate of global fossil fuel companies.

But at what cost?

For Jabirr Jabirr man Wayne Barker, 'I got a lot of heartache. Got a lot of pain. Didn't get any money. Didn't get any benefits. Got a lot of grey hairs. And I lost relationships built up over generations.'

Many of these relationships were within the Goolarabooloo and Jabirr Jabirr joint native title claim, through which the protest had driven a sharp wedge. This was disastrous for the Goolarabooloo, who were found, in the eyes of the law, not to be Traditional Owners of the land. In 2017, Justice Anthony North determined their connection to the area did not go back far enough and they did not possess native title rights or interests as defined by the *Native Title Act 1993*. Lily O'Neill, an academic who wrote extensively on James Price Point, suggested the Goolarabooloo were mistaken by many non-Aboriginal protesters as the 'true Traditional Owners' because protesters and conservation groups needed Traditional Owner support for the No Gas campaign (O'Neill 598). Had the protest not become so divisive and the in-fighting so bitter, the initial joint claim would likely have been determined.

Irene Davey was 'saddened that protesters didn't think we could make the right decisions for ourselves ... Traditional Owners got criticised so much, even though it was the government that decided it [the gas plant's location].'

Frank Parriman looked around Broome and saw a bit of pearling, a bit of hospitality, a bit of agriculture, but mostly an economy bolstered by government and welfare services. He noted it was still predominantly non-Aboriginal people employed in these services. 'Kartiya were still controlling everything. Aboriginal people didn't get a look-in. The Kimberley, and in this case, Broome, was a town where the main industry was human care services-based welfare, particularly of Aboriginal poverty and dysfunction.'

What might have been different if those so passionately opposed to the gas plant had instead demanded change to the legislation which gave Aboriginal people no veto over development? Perhaps if protesters had pressured the state government to change the *Aboriginal Heritage Act 1972* to close the loopholes which would, years later, allow for the legal destruction of one of the oldest heritage sites in the world, then Kimberley Aboriginal people might today be in a better position to say a duress-free 'no' to development, should they so choose.

In Wayne's view, the protesters' insistent and genuine plea that the Kimberley not be transformed into another Pilbara was undermined by their actions. Protesters punished Traditional Owners for demanding a seat at the negotiating table and by doing so created a Pilbara-esque situation that could have seen Traditional Owners silenced and sidelined by companies and governments, receiving no compensation, no jobs, no protection of cultural heritage, no say.

When reflecting on the Noonkanbah dispute thirty years earlier, Steve Hawke considers that it is only by asserting themselves that Aboriginal people have won ground. He suggests the frontline fighters are not always those who receive the benefits. Wayne gained nothing tangible from the years he poured into the Browse LNG Agreements. But perhaps he did win ground by raising the level of agreement-making in Australia, which might benefit other Traditional Owner groups in the unenviable position of negotiating with mining companies over access and use of land.

Former Woodside CEO Don Voelte, when he spoke with academic Lily O'Neill some years later, said of Wayne, 'I cannot believe the hell that he must have gone through. He's a big man. Wayne impacted me. In a small way, and I don't want to be misunderstood on this – you know how Nelson Mandela impacted the world ... and I don't want to embarrass Wayne, but I just want to say that it's kind of the same thing, on a smaller scale' (O'Neill 188–189).

In any case, for Wayne, it was time to move on, intellectually if not yet emotionally.

'I think I had an idealistic view of making a difference. I think now, with my knowledge, if I got offered the permanent job as CEO of KLC I would need to think long and hard about it. It's not fair that my wife, kids and family pay a price for the job I choose to do. I'm more self-aware of how to create value, more aware of only working with people who believe in you. I've got a history of sticking with things for these ten-year blocks. I think land councils require fresh blood every five to ten years. If you stay longer, you're doing Aboriginal members a disservice, because you don't perform as well.'

7: Work hard, have fun, get shit done

When Wayne jumped from chief executive of the KLC to chief executive of KRED Enterprises, his former colleagues wondered who he would 'steal' next to staff the new venture.[14] Wayne knew if KRED was to be successful, he needed to pull in a constellation of people who were loyal and trustworthy. He picked the toughest and brightest from his old team at KLC—men and women committed to self-determination and motivated to work with him on KRED's mission to create independent Aboriginal economic development. The organisation's formal tagline was 'walking in two worlds'. Among staff, the informal tagline was 'work hard, have fun, get shit done', a sentiment which had guided Wayne's dad's working life. As KRED's staff grew, its lawyers would come to refer to their boss as 'Waynestorm', a reference to the storm of ideas he would unleash on whoever happened to be first in the office. 'How'd you go getting Wayned-on?' staff would grin and ask each other over midmorning coffee.

The first to join Wayne from KLC was Jen Allen, Wayne's executive assistant. She was excited about the prospect of setting up a totally new organisation, and she loved working at Wayne's pace. 'You have to be on the ball all the time. You have to match Wayne's hours. You can't be someone who's got problems or who likes to chat rubbish.' During the gas days, her phone never left her side.

'I would have my phone on all the time, and any time he rang, I'd just pick it up straight away. I was on call every hour of the day, to the point where I'd wake up through the night, and I had a notepad by the bedside table that I'd write things down on. The reason I think I worked so well with him is because I'd be able to fill in all his gaps. He'd be talking about, say, a company, and then he'd go, *Ah, what's that woman's name...?* And then I'd put the name in there. I'd be able to fill in the missing pieces because he always worked on that huge, big picture. But yeah, it was really full on.'

The KRED office was located on the second level of a new white tin building off Dampier Terrace in Chinatown, overhanging mangroves and the turquoise swell of the spring and king tides. Staff joked about knocking the windows out of Wayne's office so they could fish during their lunch breaks. The building was in a storied part of Broome, which had once seen Japanese and Malay pearl divers camped in humpies above the high tideline. Muddy soy sauce urns and square Dutch gin bottles were still sometimes bared by the sea. While the office was on Yawuru country, the decor had strong links to the desert—vivid paintings of jilas and sand dunes. Many of the paintings were gifted to Wayne and Chris during their years in Fitzroy.

There were those who were suspicious—who suspected Wayne cared only about money and would pursue a pro-development agenda at all costs. He was exasperated by the gossip that he was 'in it for himself'. 'If I wanted to get rich, I'd already be rich. And I wouldn't be living in Broome, I'd be living in the Bahamas instead of working for Kimberley Traditional Owners!'

By establishing KRED Enterprises, Wayne saw himself as fulfilling a vision articulated by Traditional Owners at a meeting in 1991 at Rugan Community. The meeting resulted in 'The

Crocodile Hole Report', a landmark document which detailed a range of Traditional Owner aspirations, including that Aboriginal organisations work together and not let external forces divide and rule them; that Aboriginal people might run their own businesses; and that when it came to negotiations with outside stakeholders, all relevant Traditional Owners and custodians were to be present on matters of concern. Stakeholders were not to contact or negotiate through one individual. These hopes had steered Wayne during the James Price Point negotiations and would also become the bedrock of KRED's work.

In addition to 'The Crocodile Hole Report', Wayne had been influenced by the thinking of African American Muslim and polemic Malcolm X, particularly his 1964 speech 'The Ballot or the Bullet', in which he described the philosophy of black nationalism. It encompassed a belief that black people should be voting for black politicians. Wayne says, 'He talks about how when the white man comes and asks you to vote for him, it's the only time you ever see him. You need someone from your own community to be in parliament, because they're the only ones who really understand the issues.' Malcolm X also urged black people to spend their money with black-owned businesses. In Australia, Indigenous-owned businesses were over one hundred times more likely to employ Indigenous workers than white-owned businesses ('Indigenous Business' 2).

So how did KRED go about creating independent Aboriginal economic development? First, Wayne knew the organisation had to be structured in a way that was consistent with cultural values. He was only interested in working with Traditional Owners who shared his vision. Initially, six native title groups agreed to become members of KRED. The lands of these six groups stretched from the tidal turquoise creeks of Bardi Jawi country, to the cool river bends on Nykina Mangala country, to the lunar landscapes of Ngurrara country in the Great Sandy Desert. They formed the Ambooriny Burru Foundation, the social arm of the organisation, with KRED Enterprises as the economic development arm. Any surplus income made by KRED was shared between Ambooriny Burru Foundation's members. The importance of sharing was something Wayne had learned from his Nana Aggie and from the senior Traditional Owners he'd worked with during his years at the Kimberley Aboriginal Law and Culture Centre. He says, 'Aboriginal people in the Kimberley have always shared and looked after each other … KRED has a strong foundation in culture. It's about building wealth for Aboriginal people in a way which is beneficial to all of us.'

Bardi man Frank Davey, an early supporter of KRED who grew up on Sunday Island, described how, when he was a boy, he would go out with his dad and other elders spearing fish for dinner. When they came back to shore, they went around to all the different camps and asked people if they needed any extra fish. They shared everything and cared for everybody. Through KRED, Frank Davey saw a possibility to extend these values.

In the spirit of keeping these values strong, Wayne regularly brought to the KRED office a tropical bounty of bananas, mangoes and wild honey from his bees, as well as the occasional barni (goanna). The staff contributed delicacies like curried dugong and turtle, as well as jars of chilli Broome belachan made from fish, crab and pearl meat.

Wayne's generosity extended to mentorship. Ngurrara Traditional Owner Peter Murray, who was chief executive of Yanunijarra Aboriginal Corporation and served as KRED's second chairman, reflects, 'Wayne's a good listener and he looks after his team—no matter what age group. Once he invests in you, it doesn't stop ... I've found him really supportive in my role, particularly in helping grow me as a leader. A lot of his explanations about issues are scenario-based, from things that have happened, or will happen. So, he helps you understand those high-level politics. He's also a strong cultural man who practised law and culture at a young age and never let it go.'

While Wayne has practised his traditional law and culture for more than thirty years, it is not something he uses publicly as ammunition. He doesn't go around saying, 'I'm a law man.' To do so, he believes, would be belittling to what he has been taught.

The establishment of KRED was something which inspired hope in many Traditional Owners. For Gajerrong woman Merle Carter, the thing that excited her most was the possibility of being free from government control. 'Our life now is like we're stuck. We've gotta rely on government for funding. With KRED, we won't have to ... we'll be able to get control of our future and do things our way, in an Aboriginal cultural way ... I got real good binyji [feeling] that we'll have KRED there to help us deal with our social problems, with suicide, which is the main issue, and then we won't need the government. We won't need their money. Because they can't tell us what to do with it, because it's our money. It's from our organisation that's set up for the people ... this was one of the visions for the old people' (Stratton 06:48–08:37).

Joe Brown, who had worked closely with Wayne back in the KALACC days, spoke of the importance of yinyirli, meaning gifts exchanged at ceremonies, like boomerangs and clothes. Through application of cultural values, like yinyirli in a contemporary context, he hoped to see changes within the community—his particular concern was the hopelessness and trauma that led to youth suicide. 'When you get old and then you die, it should be for a proper reason. Not just taking your life.' (Stratton 14:12–29).

While KRED's work was always underpinned by negotiations, there was a time when Wayne also considered potential Aboriginal business proposals. If Kimberley Aboriginal people could *own* the remote community stores where they bought the bulk of their food, would this drive down prices? As it was, an avocado might cost seven dollars, a block of cheese ten, two litres of orange juice twelve, and a pack of freezer-burned meat over thirty. Another proposal considered the viability of farming and selling traditional bush products, like the superfood gubinge (Kakadu plum). But as the organisation grew, its focus narrowed.

Wayne had recognised a tension in KLC between its mandate to secure native title for its members and its role negotiating commercial agreements with proponents. Its lawyers were primarily trained in native title and funded by the Commonwealth. This funding dependence put KLC in a difficult position if it wished to challenge the federal government for not acting in the best interests of Traditional Owners. KRED was independent. Set up as a charitable business, it generated its own income. Its non-reliance on government funding meant it could criticise government. Under KRED, Wayne established Arma Legal, an Aboriginal-owned legal company which focused mostly on commercial agreements and Environmental Heritage and Social Impact Services (EHSIS), which could be contracted to undertake heritage, archaeological and environmental survey work ahead of any mining on traditional lands.

Its staff were buoyant and boisterous, and office banter was a lively mix of Kriol and English. Ronald Wade, a bull breeder who bitterly recalled the days he needed a 'coon-pass' to get into Broome, worked for KRED's EHSIS. On his office-based weeks, between on-country surveys, he'd perch up in front of his computer and roar, 'Divvy! Where's my rat?' Divina D'Anna, still a few years from becoming a Kimberley MP, would search the office desks for Ronald's computer mouse. Wayne's executive assistant, Amanda Gregory, was a whip-smart young Karajarri woman who effortlessly code-switched between English and Kimberley Kriol, registering with delight the surprise on the faces of industry leaders and government ministers when they came to the KRED office and realised she was Aboriginal. Wayne, along with his Aboriginal staff, came up against this inherent, subconscious racism daily.

* * *

Through KRED and Arma Legal, Wayne was able to continue the kind of maverick agreement-making which had distinguished him at the KLC. The company's lawyers were encouraged to exhaust all available legal avenues to achieve the best outcomes for Traditional Owners. Hayley Haas started working for KRED in 2012. She'd studied international criminal law in Italy and then had moved to London. There, she worked in human rights law to satisfy the heart and in commercial litigation to pay the bills. A job caught her eye when she was renewing her visa back in Australia. KRED was looking for an in-house commercial litigator—meaningful work that would still pay the bills. Hayley applied, was successful, and asked friends in London to pack her room and ship her belongings to Broome. She found working with Wayne exhilarating.

'He had an encyclopedic knowledge and a unique way of looking at negotiations, strategically speaking. He could switch between a commercial, political, legal or cultural approach at a whim—it made our job a lot easier, as it meant opposing parties couldn't get sure footing on what approach to take.'

This knowledge was built by tenacity—by Wayne's capacity to fixate on certain things. Hayley noted that sometimes this single-mindedness could pose its own challenges. One day, unhappy with his waistline, Wayne decided to go on a radical diet. He'd eat for five days of the week and starve himself for two. This went on for several months. The team learned to schedule any important meetings on the 'eating days', when his focus was sharp and his energy unmatchable. On the 'starving days' he was distracted and fatigued.

Given KRED received no government funding, it was a lean work environment. Hayley would do the drafting and fix the photocopiers. She prepared submissions in multiple formats to appease the preferences of judges whose expectations were more aligned with the productivity of large, well-resourced firms, not individual lawyers sometimes working from the back of a troopy. On evenings ahead of big authorisation meetings, she pulled all-nighters at the office, listening to the hot slap of the sea on the jetty, and the whine of midgies and mozzies.

Part of what pushed Hayley was the responsibility vested in her by Wayne.

One of her first tasks was representing Nyikina Mangala Traditional Owners in a stoush against Buru Energy Ltd. Buru had been undertaking work on its Ungani oilfield operations near a sacred site called Yilakan, or Blue Hills. The area had been a significant meeting place for Nyikina people and it still cradled an extensive array of artefacts, like grinding stones and spear-sharpening tools, as well as rock paintings containing over five thousand motifs. Buru had an agreement with Nyikina Mangala over access to the country. Part of this agreement stipulated there must be Aboriginal cultural heritage monitors present during all ground-disturbing work within a prescribed buffer zone. The monitors, two Nyikina women, Rosita and Linda, could issue a stop-work order if artefacts or cultural heritage might be damaged.

Catastrophe struck when the women were called away to a funeral.

Buru pushed ahead with its schedule, grading seismic lines through a sand dune within the buffer zone and causing irreparable cultural damage.

Wayne took Hayley to Jarlmadangah community during the sweltering start of the wet season of 2012 to discuss the issue with John Watson. Beyond the burning car windows, boabs and termite nests flashed by. Upon arrival in Jarlmadangah, Wayne, with future litigation on his mind, recalls saying to John, 'This is Hayley, Nyikina Mangala's new lawyer. She's going to be our Rottweiler. Our junkyard dog.' Hayley remembers John giving her the once-over, and a big grin. Standing there in her spectacles and floral blouse, skin still London-pale, she looked nothing like a junkyard dog![15]

In the wake of the Blue Hills disaster, several of Buru's executives and consultants fell dangerously ill or died—there was a case of encephalitis, a case of cancer, a fatal motorcycle accident. Then, in 2013, a National Native Title Tribunal member, Daniel O'Dea, found that a mining exploration licence over the same area could be granted to an explorer named Bill Richmond. This was granted through the 'expedited procedure' process, meaning the explorer wasn't required to negotiate with Traditional Owners. John was anxious that even more damage might be done to Blue Hills. In an affidavit presented to the National Native Title Tribunal he warned, 'The explorer and his workers have to be very careful, wherever you walk or damage parts of the exploration licence area someone will get sick, certain people will get sick depending on where they walk. This is what Nyikina Mangala people know to be true from our cultural heritage knowledge' (*Daisy* 19).

A few months after ruling in favour of Bill Richmond, Daniel O'Dea suffered a heart attack during Perth's City to Surf fun run. Two days later he was dead.

*　*　*

In 2014 Sheffield Resources Ltd, a mineral sands company aspiring to mine ninety-five kilometres north-east of Broome, applied for a mining lease from the Department of Mines and Petroleum. The lease covered the lands of the Mount Jowlaenga people: country wild with wattle and bloodwood, rocky outcrops and pindan, grassy plains and freshwater springs. Culturally, it was a place where groups travelled to collect ochre; historically, it had been the site of an unrecorded massacre in which one of the native title group's named applicant's great-great-grandmothers had been killed. The name of Sheffield's mine, Thunderbird, was incongruous with the country it proposed to occupy. It suggested both North American mythology and cheap American wine. One of Sheffield's neighbouring prospects, Night Train, also carried the name of a cheap wine. Tasteless, maybe, or thoughtless, in a region where alcohol had wreaked havoc on communities.

The mine was expected to operate for around forty years.

Under the *Native Title Act 1993*, parties are obliged to negotiate in 'good faith', a principle intended to give Traditional Owners the power to bargain on equal footing with proponents. Sheffield and KRED's Arma Legal had negotiated in good faith but failed to reach an agreement. Wayne says, 'Negotiations stalled because the agreement we were presented with didn't include minimum benchmark standards—standards that have been the basis of the last twenty years of best practice in agreement-making in the Kimberley.' The company was restive; negotiations had already gone on too long. Wayne recalls it 'pressed the button' on Section 35 of the Native Title Act, demanding of the National Native Title Tribunal (NNTT) a determination in relation to the mining lease.

Then it blundered. Sheffield staff went to lengths to make direct contact with the leading applicant members of the native title party, bypassing their legal representatives. They turned up in communities and waited outside funerals. Each time, they held a letter stating the offer was still on the table.

In 'The Crocodile Hole Report' there's clear condemnation of the idea of companies approaching individuals. KRED had enshrined this principle in the negotiation protocol with Sheffield. By directly contacting the Traditional Owners, Sheffield breached the good faith which had underscored negotiations up to this point. Arma Legal reported its concern to the NNTT. Wayne says it was as much about strategy as about ensuring good faith was upheld. 'Economic windows open and shut. The longer the project was delayed, the greater the risk to investors, and the more pressure on the company to meet Traditional Owner demands.'

The NNTT found Sheffield had no obligation to negotiate in good faith after making a Section 35 application. KRED then appealed to the Federal Court. The primary judge concurred with the NNTT's findings. There was one more course of action: an appeal to the Full Federal Court.

On the instruction of Traditional Owners, Hayley worked on the appeal. 'We knew we had a strong case and couldn't understand how the good faith obligation could be interpreted any differently. We were devastated by the single judge's decision. On appeal, we refined the arguments even more precisely.'

Two out of the three judges of the Full Federal Court agreed Sheffield did have a good faith obligation in negotiations they conducted after commencing a Section 35 application.

It was a satisfying victory.

'The Traditional Owners had stuck with the process for so long. They were meeting on Sundays. They were so disappointed in Sheffield's conduct. The way the Native Title Act is set up is skewed to allow for this to happen and there's no recourse to stop it from happening. We'd put so much into it and the result made us feel like the right decision does sometimes get made.'

The win sent a clear message to companies: Kimberley Traditional Owners were not pushovers. With Wayne at the helm, Arma Legal would go the whole way within the bounds of the law to pursue positive outcomes for its clients.

* * *

At Lanji Lanji, on Nyikina country, the freshwater of the Martuwarra cuts through the open plains to stir with the salt of the sea before flowing on into the King Sound near Derby. It's a nursery, where baby sawfish are born and freshwater cherrabun spawn. Bull sharks, barramundi, and crocodiles loiter in the mud-dark pools.

It was here that Nyikina and Mangala people celebrated the determination of their native title on 29 May 2014.

Wayne drove to Lanji early that morning with his family.

'I stopped and broke some branches because I knew we were going to dance Walangarri, with those spears or sticks you dance with. When we got there, everyone was getting painted up. I remember Anthony grabbed a hold of Jarred and painted him up. We wore white headbands because we see white as a neutral colour. When you put the red headband on, it signifies you're waking up more serious secret men's stuff. Our mob do it in a way so that we don't scare anyone. And that mark we do, in ochre, is a willinge, it signifies cloud ...'

Justice Gilmour—towering, black-gowned, representing the Federal Court of Australia—was welcomed to country by John Watson, singing part of the Woonyoomboo story. Nyikina men danced around the judge in one direction, Nyikina ladies in the other. As Wayne danced, he felt a profound upwelling of emotion.

'In my earlier days at the KLC, I heard some old people describe what it was like getting their native title. They said, *We're so happy, we're shining from the inside!* It was like that. I was thinking of all our senior people. I was thinking that just there, across the river at Yeeda Homestead, that was where granny [Jira] was born. I was thinking of Nana Aggie's stories, about the old people walking across the mouth of the Fitzroy River to Derby on a big springtide ... It was really important that finally, after eighteen years—we were one of the first claims lodged—it was nearly over.'

The dancers accompanied Justice Gilmour to an open-air tent where the determination was formally handed down.

Robert Watson was one of the Traditional Owners who spoke eloquently about what the determination meant to his people. He says, 'Getting native title was not only about the recognition of Aboriginal people from the area as the original inhabitants of this land, but it was also about having real control and real influence to make change for the destiny of the people in our area. We want to be sitting front and centre to determine how services are delivered and how opportunities are provided for Aboriginal people to advance themselves, not only for social change, but also for economic development. They both go hand in hand.'

It wasn't an easy journey to get to this point. Robert says the whole native title process—of proving your connection to country—had a terrible impact on Nyikina families. 'Some families had more knowledge than others. If you don't have any knowledge, are you a Traditional Owner? Maybe not, according to the law. This created a community dynamic which was very, very taxing, costly, painful and soul degrading. My view has always been that we shouldn't penalise people because they are victims of circumstances or because they were exposed to the maximum impact of dispossession. It's really important we embrace and try to reconnect families through their connection to country.'

After the dust from the dancers and the day settled, Wayne, too, felt somewhat let down by the vision of native title, and the reality.

'I remember back in my early days, when I was twenty-one years old, sitting on the oval in Fitzroy Crossing when Peter Yu was chief executive of the Land Council. The government was looking to shape the Native Title Bill. I remember Peter was seeking instructions from everyone present. We broke into men's groups and women's groups. And we all came forward with the issues that were important to us, what we wanted to see in the Act. To us, native title meant rights, sovereignty, control. But what we have today is a mere glimmer, a mere glimpse of the aspirations of those warriors and agitators who raised their voices for better rights. This is not reflected in how native title runs now, that's for sure.'

Robert also doesn't believe native title has delivered what was hoped.

'No way at all. We're still banging our heads against a wall.'

* * *

At KRED's peak in 2014 and 2015, it employed 226 people. Two hundred and sixteen of those were Aboriginal. Most were employed on a casual basis to accompany mining companies on cultural heritage surveys. KRED received no government funding and was running as a successful Indigenous business. In 2016, Wayne engaged a consultant to undertake an economic impact assessment on KRED's activities. He found that KRED had contributed just over twenty-four million dollars to the Kimberley regional economy and had provided over eleven thousand hours of pro bono work for Traditional Owners. This was no small feat given its work spanned some of the most remote parts of Australia and employed people from some of the most remote communities.

The successes were also extraordinary in that they occurred during a time of intense uncertainty for Kimberley Traditional Owners. In 2014, WA Premier Colin Barnett threatened to close more than half of Western Australia's remote Aboriginal communities by cutting off essential services like power and water. The federal government weighed into the debate, with Prime Minister Tony Abbott announcing that taxpayers should not have to fund people's 'lifestyle choices' (Medhora). No thought was given to the right of people to live on their traditional country, for which they had ancient and deep responsibilities, nor to the fact that many of the communities were alcohol-free at the direction of their leaders, nor to the fact that previous government policies which saw people shunted from their traditional lands had been disastrous. Wayne, through his business savvy at KRED, was proving that jobs *could* be created for people on their traditional lands. He was proving that life in remote communities—obviously spiritually viable—could also be economically viable.

The Kimberley Land Council's CEO, Nolan Hunter, and chair, Anthony Watson, raised the issue at the United Nations Permanent Forum on Indigenous Issues in New York and reprehended the Australian Government for its systemic interference with attempts by Indigenous people to pursue culturally appropriate economic development opportunities. After national and international condemnation, the government back-pedalled from its threat.

Then Western Australia's mining boom went bust.

It was 2016 and thousands found themselves without work. With the downward trend in exploration and mining, KRED was also facing increasing financial stress. Chief Financial Officer Jodie Pincini says, 'We'd been set up during the boom and now, all of a sudden, there were staff sitting around doing nothing.'

Wayne knew the only way to stay on track was to issue redundancies. Five of the staff were given curt, typed letters and two weeks notice. The office air was riven with disbelief. There were bills to be paid, families to be fed. There were tears. Jodie recalls, 'Wayne had wanted to go early and hard because he could see how quickly things were going to turn. I was reluctant and thought we had to be a little bit careful. In hindsight, we could have saved a lot of money … if I had listened, we would have been better off financially. But it's so hard, letting staff go.'

KRED scaled back to focus solely on core business. It had always been a lean work environment—now it was leaner still. Energy was put into ensuring EHSIS and Arma Legal could make a profit and be self-sufficient. But the office was quieter, the mood sombre, the jokes fewer.

The remaining staff were fearful they might be next.

Nationally, things weren't much brighter. In May 2017, Aboriginal and Torres Strait Islander delegates from around Australia convened at Uluru, where they released the Uluru Statement from the Heart. The Statement called for the establishment of a First Nations Voice enshrined in the Constitution and a Makarrata Commission to supervise a process of agreement-making between governments and First Nations and to oversee truth-telling about history.

Wayne had been involved in the process as part of a forum in Broome, and then as chair of the landmark meeting. He says, 'The Statement is a principle document: it's about voice, treaty and truth. I remember talking about truth-telling as being fundamental because I've read and seen the work of Nelson Mandela, and the work of the Archbishop Desmond Tutu. To be able to move on, to heal, the absolute raw truth has to be told. We don't need to forgive anyone, but we do need to be heard about what happened.'

Prime Minister Malcolm Turnbull's government rejected the call for a Voice to Parliament, in what senior Indigenous leaders and legal voices described as 'a despicable act of mean-spirited bastardry' (Wahlquist). A year later, Morrison's government followed suit, claiming an Indigenous voice would constitute a 'third chamber' of parliament and making it clear it wasn't interested in a referendum to enshrine a voice into the Constitution (Karp). To Wayne, it seemed like an egregious lack of leadership from the nation's prime ministers.

'Both governments' responses show the nature of politics is about staying in power and staying popular. But sometimes the justice that's required is not popular. Keating championed the

Native Title Act. It was not a popular decision for him, but it was the right thing to do.'

It had been a stormy few years for Kimberley Traditional Owners.

For Wayne, things were about to get worse.

Personal.

His eldest daughter was about to be publicly attacked.

8: Judge, jury and executioner

'What's a podcast?'

Some of the old people were weeping, some were fretful, some were frightened. 'What's this about a podcast?' they asked at the Kimberley Land Council's 2018 AGM. 'We've heard some kartiya bin asking around, running down Land Council, asking about law …'

Wayne recalls hearing 'a rumour someone was about to do a number on Anthony Watson and myself'.

It wasn't a rumour.

Richard Baker, a Walkley Award–winning journalist from Melbourne's *The Age*, had been interviewing people for his podcast *Wrong Skin*. The podcast sought to investigate the disappearance of a young man and woman from Nyikina country during the wet season of 1994.

Episode one opened with a braid of human knuckles—the young woman's knuckles—found in a bowerbird nest near the community of Looma. In setting the scene, Baker described the Kimberley as 'seductive' but tempered this with the observation 'it feels as though it could turn on you at any minute' (Baker Episode One 02:25). In his eyes, admittedly the eyes of a non-Aboriginal outsider, the wet season was 'a spectacular but dangerous time' (Baker Episode One 02:14).

Right from the opening Wayne felt a prickling, nape-of-the-neck warning. For him, the wet season was not a time fraught with danger but a time of renewal. 'It's a time when the billabongs fill up with water, the goannas start getting fat and the ducks come into season. It's a time of new life; it's a good time.'

What Wayne found dangerous was not the promise of rain but the Western cultural prism through which his country was being described and judged.

Listeners were introduced to two young people suspected of falling in love the 'wrong way'. They belonged to the same skin group, making a relationship under traditional law forbidden. Julie Buck was twenty-three and had been promised as a wife to an older man. Richard Milgin was twenty-four, and it's his mum, Annie Milgin, who tells the story of how Woonyoomboo made Nyikina country at the start of this book. The couple went missing in January 1994. Only Julie was found—first her body, partially clothed in a denim skirt, then later her knuckles.

Baker said the couple appear to have paid dearly for wanting to be together and intimated they were murdered in tribal punishment. He suggested Annie's husband, John Watson, and John's son, chair of the Kimberley Land Council Anthony Watson, were perhaps complicit, perhaps knew something.

These inferences put a terrible strain on the family. Anthony, who had served as KRED Enterprises' first chairperson and was serving as chair of the Kimberley Land Council, says, 'I felt really gutted. People who were making those allegations lied in the public domain and got away with it. Those stories were not accurate or true. It drove us to madness. To be cast around Australia … Richard Baker was tricky and selective with his words, not saying we were murderers, but saying we should know things about it. It was unfair journalism and it made us angry.'

Anthony says the allegations in the podcast undermined Aboriginal leadership.

'There was a political agenda to remove us from the work that we've done. If you see our record toward responsible development, our stance on heritage, on the Fitzroy River, the work we've done for native title—helping people from the desert to the coast have their native title recognised—this is our lifetime work toward self-determination. But I nearly lost my career. Every time a new episode was broadcast, more allegations mounted up against us. My chairmanship, my employment at the land council, was in jeopardy.'

The podcast also deepened old and complex family and community rifts. Even prior to the podcast Anthony says, 'It wasn't comfortable for Dad in the community. I told Dad and my sisters and my family to move to Broome, away from Jarlmadangah. The podcast contributed to it; it was a major issue.'

Baker believes his distance from the local politics, his position as an outsider, gave him a unique vantage point from which to tell Julie and Richard's story. 'Sometimes it takes an outsider to fully ventilate these things that have been going on as undercurrents. That's the world up there, and it's hard to escape it [if you're from that world], because you've got to live with and get along with people. I was actually trying to open a window onto that world—without making it a horror show—and I think the Australian media has a huge obligation to get out there in the real world and explore these issues.'

Wayne had a different take on the subject matter and the journalist's approach. 'The podcast embodied those early perceptions of Aboriginal people as primitive. Baker told this story from the perspective of the dominant culture. He might not think he's racist, but he has set himself up as the jury, judge and executioner of his own point of view. This kind of cultural superiority has soured Aboriginal and non-Aboriginal relations in the Kimberley since colonisation.'

* * *

By Episode Five the podcast had swerved from the story of Richard and Julie to fixate on Wayne, Wayne's daughter Sara, and KRED Enterprises. Wayne found the jump in subject matter baffling. He'd never heard of the couple's ill-starred story prior to the podcast, had no connection to the case, and had no idea why he was in Baker's gunsight. It seems Baker was keen to home in on a 'widespread belief that the same people keep winning, while others are left behind' (Baker Episode Five 08:33). This was in the context of native title and those Traditional Owners unhappy with the KLC and native title processes.

Wayne was identified as one of the winners. He was accused of real or perceived conflicts of interest, given the relationship between the KLC and KRED. Baker argued that the KLC had outsourced the profitable parts of native title to KRED. He claimed Wayne's salary was $450 an hour, that Wayne and KRED held 'enormous power' over the fortunes of ASX-listed companies, and that a petition from Looma and Noonkanbah Traditional Owners seeking to remove KRED as their representative had been lodged with the federal government.

KRED swiftly set the record straight.

The claim of outsourcing implied wrongdoing, whereas in fact outsourcing work in relation to future acts is provided for under the Native Title Act. In Wayne's view, it was better this work go to a local Indigenous organisation, a charity, rather than lining the pockets of non-Indigenous lawyers and consultants. Wayne's charge-out rate to mining companies was not what he received from KRED—his salary was much lower. And even if it was, Wayne felt there was unconscious bias in the comment. Was he, an Aboriginal person, not worth this much? He wondered how likely it would be for Baker to query the hourly rate of a white chief executive officer. The comment relating to Looma and Noonkanbah Traditional Owners had no basis in fact—KRED had never represented these groups. And Baker's statement about the 'enormous power' Wayne and KRED wielded was laughable, given the appalling power imbalance between billion-dollar ASX-listed companies and Traditional Owners.

Considering this so-called 'enormous power', Wayne says, 'Everyone seems to think I've got all this power. I don't understand why that is. Is it because I know how to get shit done? All the old people, they ring me to sort out problems. I sort them out. The value of leadership in the Kimberley is if the leader is put under pain and pressure, then people have more respect ... But ultimately, if what you're doing is right, and people don't like it, this doesn't matter. You have to keep doing it.'

Wayne was no stranger to public attacks.

'I've spent the majority of my life fighting for the rights of Traditional Owners. This has put me in the firing line. But I chose this job, I chose this political path. My family did not. That's where Baker went next.'

* * *

When Sara was nineteen she graduated from the Dreamtime Project, an initiative focused on building leadership and confidence in young Aboriginal women through fashion. She was subsequently selected along with eleven other young Aboriginal women to attend a modelling and cultural exchange to New York. The girls were encouraged to approach businesses and companies from their local area to seek sponsorship for the trip. Dreamtime Project's manager, Sylvia Giacci, provided them with a formal letter detailing the project and outlining their request. The girls then wrote cover emails.

In *Wrong Skin* an actor read part of Sara's email. Baker stated this email was sent to mining companies KRED was working with, and suggested Sara was attempting to use her dad's influence for her own gain.

He didn't mention the sponsorship request came from the Dreamtime Project, not Sara.

He didn't mention, when musing 'how many other young people in the Kimberley would even be in a position to try such a thing on?' that eleven other young Aboriginal women were also seeking sponsorship (Baker Episode Five 37:17).

He didn't contextualise the numerous requests for sponsorship mining companies receive—from football teams to community arts centres—or the blind and desperate dependence of small communities on such funding.

Wayne says, 'What he did do was expose Sylvia Giacci to fraud by publishing her signature online. This was later removed, but the false claims about Sara were not.'

Sara's request for sponsorship was unsuccessful.

In the podcast Baker tells the audience he thought hard about whether to include her. He decided Sara's letter illustrated Wayne's power, his status as a 'winner', and exemplified a potential conflict-of-interest situation which served the broader point of the episode.

'This was a long bow to draw. Baker didn't make it clear to me that he was going to attack Sara, and he made no attempt to contact Sara regarding his allegations,' Wayne says.

When Sara learned of her inclusion in the podcast and accompanying news article she was 'wild'. 'My whole life I have been the goody-two-shoes. I've never done anything that could be interpreted as wrong or posted anything inappropriate online. Because Dad has such a high public profile I've always known that if I fuck up, it reflects badly on him. I'm always careful to think about other people, my family, before I make decisions. Not once did it cross my mind that Dad's work might somehow involve me.'

Sara said the podcast took an especially heavy toll on her dad.

'It was keeping him up at night, it was making him sick, it was causing him so much stress. I knew this was about protecting me, because Dad's never been one to care what people say about him. The journalist made it personal by bringing the people Dad cares about into it. When I read it [the article], all I could see were lies. The people who are important know this is all lies.'

The article carried the headline 'Native Entitlement: Wheeling and Dealing in the Kimberley' (Baker). Wayne was ropeable when he considered the connotations of the headline. 'Did Baker mean to suggest native title was an entitlement? Was he referring to my daughter as a "native" with what could be perceived as a sense of entitlement?'

Wayne thought about the way the word 'native' had been used

historically: in the journals of Mjöberg, the annual reports from Beagle Bay Mission, the legislation that curtailed the rights of his ancestors. He thought about the podcast, the factual inaccuracies and the lack of understanding about the division between those who followed law and culture and those who followed God. He thought about the old bitter grudge between Looma and Jarlmadangah, which the podcast had served to fuel.

Wayne had initially refused Baker's requests for an interview, fearful of a hatchet job. Now, aggrieved at the inclusion of his daughter, he decided to go public, accusing *Wrong Skin* of racism for publishing his charge-out rate to companies.

Baker denies the accusation of racism. 'This is where Wayne lets himself down. He resorts to that cheap card of racism and by doing so actually does himself and his daughter a disservice. I think it reflects really badly on him. And if he has to resort to that, I might have hit a raw nerve …'

Baker didn't think Sara's inclusion in the podcast would be a 'destructive thing to do'.

'They didn't like it, and I won't be getting Christmas cards for it, but I didn't think it would be life-changing. I could have been unfair to Sara, but again, I can't change that now, and that's why it would have been good to have a proper interview [with Wayne].'

* * *

Wrong Skin earned national and international acclaim, winning the Podcasting Quill in the 2018 Quill Awards for Excellence in Victorian Journalism, as well as the inaugural Podcast of the Year and the Investigative Journalism and True Crime awards in the

2019 Australian Podcast Awards. It also won gold in the Personal Lives Podcast category at the New York Festivals Radio Awards. The accolades allowed Baker and his team to shine up their CVs.

But back in the Kimberley, while the podcast prompted a reopening of Julie and Richard's cases, and while a broad enquiry was conducted by the WA Cold Case Homicide squad, not enough evidence emerged to criminally charge any suspect. The families and friends of Julie and Richard were still in the dark. In Baker's view, the podcast ultimately had a positive impact for the friends and families of the couple. 'Siblings or family members that I was dealing with felt their story was put on the map and was no longer taboo, in terms of *hush, hush, we can't go there*.'

For Wayne, the podcast was anything but positive—he saw it as a colonial representation, as cashing in on Aboriginal people's trauma. 'If you're going to work on these kinds of stories, you need to be good at your research. You're talking to vulnerable people with deep trauma. People's brains are suspicious—toxic stress in childhood wires people's brains for protection. There's very little trust in the Kimberley.

'The science around intergenerational trauma is really clear: people who have endured early-childhood trauma have changes in the architecture of their brains. We develop brains that are adapted to survive, to protect ourselves. As with disadvantaged Indigenous people around the world, we are on constant high alert, looking for anything suspicious or dangerous. It is an incredibly difficult space to work in, as no-one trusts anyone. We have had to become like this to survive the atrocities we have endured. It has kept our people alive, but now it also works to keep us divided. This suspicion is then passed on generation to generation.'

In Wayne's view, this is something journalists need to be aware of when working in the Kimberley. 'Journalists shouldn't use this suspicion to their advantage. It is very easy to walk into the Kimberley and ask if anyone has a problem with those holding positions of power. Anyone in a position of power will always be suspected to be corrupt, no matter how honest they are. In terms of *Wrong Skin*, Baker's lack of awareness of the effects of long-term intergenerational trauma has perpetuated further trauma on the very people he thought he was fighting for. Marriages were destroyed, people had to leave their homelands. Thanks to Baker, the world now thinks Aboriginal people in power are corrupt. He didn't leave the Kimberley a better place. He walked in, played on people's suspicions, and now he has his lovely, shiny trophies, earned through bad research and untruths.'

The other issue, for both Wayne and Anthony, was the false allegations that remained public. Anthony says, 'We really wanted to sue Richard Baker, but we didn't have the funds. We raised the initial funds to get the legal advice, but it would've been a couple of hundred thousand to take it through court. We never had the funds, and then Dad [John Watson] had to withdraw that process and let it lapse. Because we're not rich. We couldn't challenge it. The people who made those allegations, they should apologise. They've hurt us very badly and had no proof.'

Wayne, too, was worried the lies about himself and KRED would stick. He issued Fairfax with a 'concerns notice' regarding the defamatory imputations in the article and podcast. The concerns notice stated that in its ordinary meaning, one could assume Wayne was corrupt. Apart from this notice, Wayne couldn't take matters further, didn't have the money to clear his name.

The podcast continued to haunt Wayne two years later. His name raised a red flag when he was trying to secure a sponsorship arrangement for his newspaper *National Indigenous Times*. The sponsorship would enable the newspaper to create cadetships for Indigenous journalists. But when the potential sponsor's compliance team undertook a due diligence check, it was alarmed by an 'adverse media article'—Baker's 'Native Entitlement'. They requested Wayne respond to the veracity of the allegations.

'Make no mistake,' Wayne says, 'this was not a romantic story about love and intrigue, about two cultures clashing. This was a journalist who first created the tar for his brush and then painted us with that tar. This was about pulling down Aboriginal leadership. Dragging us down, for his own benefit. The worst thing is, he has never corrected the facts and he has continued to reap the rewards of not telling the truth.'

Wayne wasn't the only Aboriginal businessman in Western Australia to pique Baker's interest. A few years earlier, Clinton Wolf had come under Baker's scrutiny for his involvement in the negotiation of a mining agreement with Western Desert Lands Aboriginal Corporation.

Like Wayne, Clinton felt he often had a target on his back.

Like Wayne, he was furious Baker was 'acting as judge, jury and executioner by manipulating the narrative to suit his own agenda'.

* * *

Wayne and Clinton had first met at Murdoch University as law students in 1994. Clinton recalls, 'I was flitting in and out. Wayne was actually studying. He was the same as he is now. Really studious, diligent, thoughtful and responsible. I was the complete opposite.'

While at university they teamed up with Cameron Syme, who would later become one of the lead negotiators for KLC in the Browse Agreements, and Nellie Green, a gifted Yamatji painter working at the Kulbardi Aboriginal Centre at Murdoch University. The quartet established a company called Black Ochre Arts and Nellie designed a Christmas card set. The cards were luminous, with stunning colours. But Wayne, Clinton and Cameron lacked the motivation to properly market and sell the product.

They gave the cards back to Nellie.

She had no trouble selling the lot and this prompted Clinton to consider it a business opportunity they should have stuck with.

Clinton went on to serve as chief executive of Yamatji Marlpa Aboriginal Corporation. Upon finishing university, Wayne applied for a job in Yamatji's legal department. Clinton considered his application and thought, *No way. He'll knock me off my perch.* 'I did the dirty on him and advised the legal department not to hire him. A few years later we knocked up again, this time over Kimberley Diamond Company. We weren't best friends, or close friends. You couldn't say we were brothers at that stage ...'

Clinton was representing the mining company, and Wayne, then chief executive of the KLC, was representing the mob. Wayne says, 'We were sworn enemies. I squeezed him as hard as I could.'

Nonetheless, the two men had a grudging, growing respect for each other.

A few years further on they joined forces to run Aboriginal Maritime Limited (AML), an Indigenous labour hire company servicing the maritime industries out of Darwin. At the time, there were plenty of Indigenous land-based companies, but no-one else was providing employment pathways for Aboriginal people to work at sea. Clinton admired Wayne's ability to manage several crises at once and still make a profit. He admired the fact that all of Wayne's companies boasted incredibly high Indigenous employment.

Not long after Baker's story involving Clinton in 2015, the two men spoke to each other over the phone.

Wayne says, 'Clinton and I had a conversation about how some journalists were attacking us and how we had no way to tell our story. About how when we did speak to journalists, they didn't understand Aboriginal issues. It was incredibly difficult, if not impossible, to get our story told. Clinton said, *Let's buy our own paper*.'

The newspaper *National Indigenous Times* had been put up for sale by administrators earlier in 2015. In 2016, the two, along with the late Tony Barrass, purchased the business. They transformed it into an online news site. Many of the stories spotlighted Indigenous achievement—unusual in a news landscape bleak with stories about Aboriginal disadvantage.

Journalists were also tasked with working on exclusives close to the hearts of their bosses.

One of the stories close to Wayne's heart involved a Chinese-owned pastoral lease covering Yakka Munga Station on Nyikina country. Shanghai CRED owned the lease and a division of the company, Zenith Australia Investment Holding, had been clearing land in violation of their Indigenous Land Use Agreement. *National Indigenous Times* was first to break the story. The publicity put pressure on the company to stop work until the issue had been resolved.

Wayne was fond of repeating the saying: Never pick a fight with a man who buys ink by the barrel and paper by the ton. Through *National Indigenous Times* he could draw attention to abuses suffered by Traditional Owners at the hands of companies, governments and kartiyas. By doing so he could effect change.

Wayne and Clinton worked well together, fluidly, and eventually they became the sole shareholders of the paper, meaning it now had one hundred percent Indigenous ownership. Clinton says that at the newspaper's heart there is a deep commitment to truth and righting wrongs, a commitment embodied in Wayne's day-to-day bearing.

'One thing you're going to get from Wayne is the truth. Some people like hearing it. And some don't.'

9: 'You're blackfellas, you can't run a property.'

Outside the media business and the resources sector, Wayne had been pouring hours of his time into another project to fulfil a vision articulated by Traditional Owners decades earlier.

Nationally and globally there had been an uptick of interest in cattle. Wayne had chaired the Expert Indigenous Working Group appointed to assist a Council of Australian Governments (COAG) investigation into Indigenous land administration and use, the federal government had released a white paper on developing Northern Australia (in which pastoral lease security and efficiency were key features), and a rising middle class in Indonesia and China had a growing appetite for Australian beef. Some cattle stations in the Kimberley were already Aboriginal-owned. This got Wayne thinking.

In 2002, senior Nyikina Mangala people, including Nana Aggie, had expressed a vision to see Myroodah Station handed back to Traditional Owners and operating as one entity with Mount Anderson, Lulugui and Mowla Bluff. 'We want to run the Station as a successful cattle business and we want to bring our people back to their country by establishing a Community at Myroodah. Most of all, we want to see our young people learning the business under competent managers then moving into management themselves as they learn the new ways of the pastoral industry' ('Shoulder' 1).

Wayne saw the potential of a group of Aboriginal-owned stations operating under a single management structure. He met with the Aboriginal owners of Mount Anderson, Frazier Downs and Bohemia Downs to gauge if there was interest in working together to take advantage of the economies of scale offered by an integrated pastoral enterprise.

How might this look?

The cattle could be moved between stations to prevent overgrazing, and infrastructure could be shared. One station might be used for breeding, another for fattening and finishing, a third for export. The stations would be able to turn a larger profit and employ more Traditional Owners on country if they were working together. It was from these discussions that the Kimberley Agriculture and Pastoral Company (KAPCO) was born, an organisation grounded in the cultural principles of working together, standing together and sharing.

With three initial stations committed to the venture, Wayne then turned his attention to Myroodah, where his great-grandfather Yoolya had worked at the bottom sheep camp and where his Nana Aggie had served under Harold Godbehear's wife in the kitchen. Myroodah had been purchased by the Indigenous Land Corporation (ILC) in 1999. ILC had committed to divest the station to the Nyikina Mangala Pastoral Aboriginal Corporation once business arrangements between the two groups had been clarified. ILC's board requested a report on options for these arrangements, which Traditional Owners promptly submitted.

Upon sighting the report, ILC decided the Nyikina Mangala Traditional Owners were unable to meet divestment requirements.

For Nyikina man Robert Watson, ILC's response was a 'kick in the teeth'. He says, 'They never had the intention, ever, of handing it over to Traditional Owners. I feel like ILC really played a role in destroying me as a person. Everything I'd worked to achieve to that point, including running a station of my own, all the strategic thinking that went into our vision, all those consultations with the old people ... we were led up the garden path. The Aboriginal managers around that time, right across the Kimberley, were really strong cattlemen and all they needed was that technical input. They could do the logistical management of cattle and all the hard work, they just needed the engine room and the expertise to make it all work. Nearly all businesses have an element of outsourcing to acquire the expertise required. There was no reason we couldn't have done that.'

ILC didn't think so. It kept the station in its clutches for nearly two decades.

Until Wayne turned his attention to the problem.

Myroodah would make a perfect fourth addition to KAPCO's properties. It would be the centrepiece.

* * *

The Indigenous Land Corporation was established in 1995 as part of the Keating government's response to the Mabo judgement, which had successfully overturned the myth that Australia, at the time of colonisation, was terra nullius. The response involved introducing the *Native Title Act 1993*, creating an Indigenous Land Fund to buy land for Indigenous groups (the ILC was set up under this), and implementing a social justice package (this never eventuated). After ten years, ILC was to pay for its operation and land purchases from the land fund's earnings. Its purpose was to assist Aboriginal and Torres Strait Islander people to acquire land and to manage Indigenous-held land to provide economic, environmental, social or cultural benefits.

But it became untethered from this purpose.

Its focus shifted to running commercial activities and emphasising employment and training over divestment.

Come 2009, Traditional Owners of Myroodah and Udialla stations were frustrated at the lack of progress toward divestment. They felt they were unable to meet divestment requirements because they didn't have the resources to produce business plans, didn't have proper training, and because there was inadequate communication of ILC's benchmarks. In one instance, ILC provided funds to help with a business plan. But when the business plan was found to be inadequate, there were no further funds available to revise it. Why hadn't ILC taken an ongoing supportive role to develop Traditional Owner capacity?

ILC's Western Division Manager responded to these complaints by stating the application process wasn't too difficult for people aspiring to run a pastoral station. The process was a means of indicating ability and commitment. He felt ILC's preferred divestment strategy in the Kimberley had been difficult to apply, in part, because the management capacity of the affected Aboriginal groups was inadequate. ILC decided concentration on training was 'appropriate at this stage' (Sullivan 14).

Wayne reckoned this was code for 'You're blackfellas, you can't run a property'.

* * *

Wayne began dealing with ILC in 2017 and, like the senior people before him, he found straight communication with the organisation difficult.

'ILC were the biggest snake-oil salesmen. They were running Myroodah without the support or guidance of Traditional Owners, and as a result, we had lost nearly twenty years of opportunity to build our capacity. When it came to the divestment of Myroodah, ILC conceded to handing back the land and infrastructure if we bought the stock—which was valued at 11.5 million dollars. They didn't think we'd be able to raise that capital. Reading between the lines, I don't think they had any intention of handing back the land.'

Paying for Myroodah's stock was something Wayne found galling.

'I knew the Indigenous Land Fund was set up for our benefit. In trust for us. So, to be made buy back the cattle—assets that should be considered part of the government's broad social justice response—was gut-wrenching.'

Not to be deterred, Wayne approached the Chinese.

'We were looking for investors. We weren't discriminating against anyone—be they black, brown or brindle. And the Chinese didn't discriminate against us. They were happy to sit down and have conversations, whereas Australian investors were often fundamentally racist. They wouldn't invest in an Aboriginal-owned business.'

Wayne initially had promising discussions with the ASF Group, a company interested in investment opportunities in both China and Australia.

'Unfortunately, we couldn't find the right balance between the amount of control shared between parties. They wanted total control.'

So he turned closer to home, striking a deal to borrow the money from the Commonwealth Bank and Indigenous Business Australia, with surety from Fitzroy Crossing's Aboriginal-owned Marra Worra Worra. In a banking 'first', an 11.5 million dollar loan was granted to Traditional Owners to buy the stock. ILC now had no choice. It had to divest the property.

Wayne was elated, emotional. Three generations of his family had worked on Myroodah for white bosses. There'd been his great-great-grandmother Wadadarl Brumby, her son Yoolya (Fulgentius), and Wayne's Nana Aggie. Now the pastoral lease was firmly back in the hands of his people.

For Robert, too, the divestment was momentous. 'We talk about indentured labour. My grandfather was smack bang in the middle of that and so was my dad. The trajectory it sent us on—we were part of the establishment of the economy for non-Indigenous people. We were never a priority to government or anyone else. Because we just existed on the side of society and were used when we were needed for the practical labour. There was never any plan for Aboriginal people to have success running businesses until recently.'

KAPCO's property portfolio now covered over seven hundred thousand hectares of the Kimberley.

With the company well established and Wayne nearing the ten-year mark with KRED Enterprises, the fifty-two-year-old was ready for a new challenge.

An opportunity soon arose.

Mining giant Rio Tinto had just blown up an ancient Aboriginal heritage site. One of its executives reached out to Wayne: Rio was hoping he could help the company make amends.

10: A mind endlessly restless

You couldn't just bomb the Pyramids of Giza. You couldn't just detonate the Acropolis. You couldn't just blitz the temple complex at Angkor Wat. But when it came to the destruction of Aboriginal heritage sites in Western Australia pre-dating these world-wonders by tens of thousands of years, you could basically do what you wanted under the *Aboriginal Heritage Act 1972*.

On 24 May 2020, Rio Tinto knowingly and legally blew up a forty-six-thousand-year-old rock shelter site at Juukan Gorge in the Pilbara—Juukan 2 was assessed as being of 'the highest archaeological significance in Australia' (*Never Again* vi). The caves were on the lands of the Puutu Kunti Kurrama and Pinikura peoples and contained a 'museum of heritage', including a four-thousand-year-old belt of plaited human hair that linked the site directly to the ancestors of the Traditional Owners, a pollen record charting thousands of years of environmental changes, and a grinding stone dated to thirty thousand years (*Never Again* 2).

Had Wayne's Spanish-speaking great-grandfather Yoolya still been alive, he would have known that 'rio tinto' meant 'red river'; an apt name, considering the rivers of iron ore the company was bleeding from the land.

The Juukan Gorge incident arose when Rio muscled ahead with its Brockman 4 mine expansion. Traditional Owners weren't informed of three other options for the expansion, which would have caused less impact on heritage. Instead, Rio applied for a Section 18 under the Act, admitting its plan would inevitably cause heritage damage and seeking ministerial consent to proceed. The Western Australian minister in charge of the sign-off [in 2013], a member of the Barnett government, Peter Collier, was 'apparently unaware of the significance of the site' (*Inquiry* 38).

When news of the destruction made headlines, shareholders were shocked.

The company's reputation was shattered.

Wayne was unsurprised. 'I'm reading about discoveries in London where they're digging up Roman archaeological sites from the last two thousand years and celebrating how important this history is … at the same time, here in Australia, a company blasts a forty-six-thousand-year-old heritage site, showing complete disdain for Aboriginal people and showing how little it values its relationships with Aboriginal people.'

Part of Rio Tinto's damage control was to determine whether native title holders (with which the company had agreements) would support the establishment of an Indigenous advisory group. The company asked Wayne if he might be interested in conducting the consultations. After some deliberation he told Rio that he was.

'I loved the work, it was good catching up with all the Pilbara mob, it was like dealing with the mob from the Kimberley. We'd all suffered the same things, though they'd been affected by over fifty years of mining conditioning. The Traditional Owner communities were overwhelmingly supportive of an advisory group—no-one rejected the idea. And I felt good about the engagement, about the integrity the staff at the time were presenting to me. I had the opportunity to influence change for the better at Rio. But like all advisors, you can see the problem, but it is up to the company to decide whether they will fix it. Rio took parts of my report and established an Australian advisory board.'

In the wake of Juukan Gorge, the company issued public apologies, acknowledged its failure to adequately communicate with Traditional Owners, and overhauled its board.

These gestures wouldn't prevent a Juukan Gorge from happening again.

What might, was a total revamp of the Aboriginal Heritage Act.

* * *

The former minister for Aboriginal affairs, Ben Wyatt, had announced a review of the Act in 2018. The KLC called for a whole deck of changes, including that miners may not make applications to damage, destroy, conceal or alter Aboriginal sites, and that native title holders may seek a review of decisions made under the Act. It suggested the new legislation incorporate several articles from the United Nations Declaration on the Rights of Indigenous Peoples, including the principle that the state should consult and cooperate in good faith with Indigenous peoples through their own representative institutions 'in order to obtain their free, prior and informed consent before adopting and implementing legislative or administrative measures that may affect them' (*Review* 3).

In a media release, KLC's then-acting CEO Tyronne Garstone said, 'Currently, the Act is primarily directed at processes that provide for damage to and destruction of Aboriginal sites. Applications to damage or destroy Aboriginal sites are almost never rejected' ('KLC Calls').

The new Aboriginal Cultural Heritage Bill was introduced to the Parliament of Western Australia at the end of 2021.

It was met with dismay, derision and disappointment from many Aboriginal and non-Aboriginal people working in the field. An open letter to Premier Mark McGowan—signed by land council bosses, Aboriginal heritage experts, archaeologists, anthropologists, scientists and lawyers—stated the signatories did not believe the Bill would 'recognise, protect and preserve Aboriginal cultural heritage' ('Eminent Australians'). Under the new legislation, the minister for Aboriginal affairs had the ability to approve the destruction of cultural heritage when parties were unable to reach an agreement. It put heritage protection in the hands of the government of the day—not the hands of Aboriginal people. Further, there was no appeal mechanism to challenge the minister's decision.

Wayne penned a stinging opinion piece for *National Indigenous Times*. He opened the piece by reflecting on the pastoral work he'd done when he was young, alongside whitefellas who referred to Aboriginal men, regardless of their age, as 'boy'. '*Hey boy, did you do this or that?* they'd say … All the Indigenous men would respond, *Yes boss, okay boss*' (Bergmann 'Opinion').

Wayne saw the Bill as reinforcing the racist system that had been forced upon him and his ancestors on the pastoral stations.

'It creates a decision-making process where the Minister can make decisions based on their own political interest for the State of Western Australia. It makes First Nations People compete with industry and developers to win the Minister's 'good will' for protection [of] what is important to us, as a people … A master-and-subordinate relationship. It is a relationship where we, as First Nations People, ask the Minister, *Yes boss, can you protect my* culture, my heritage, my values?' To which he can say, *Yes boy*, or *no boy*, or *yes girl*, or *no girl*. This is the power being reinforced in the new Aboriginal Heritage Act' (Bergmann 'Opinion').

Laureate Professor Peter Veth, an eminent archaeologist at the University of Western Australia and signatory of the open letter to Premier McGowan, considered the new legislation an improvement but still deficient in several crucial areas. 'It falls short in terms of the United Nations compliance, it falls short in terms of giving Traditional Owners the basic right of appeal, and it falls short in terms of national standards … The lack of national standards is shocking—we have them for aeroplanes, doctors, air-conditioning, but we don't have them for heritage!'

Given McGowan's Labor government controlled both houses of parliament, it had the opportunity to be bold—to introduce legislation which would benefit generations of Aboriginal people. But its approach was conservative. In Professor Veth's view, 'I don't think the government is going to look back on it with pride. It makes me think there's extraordinary pressure on the government from the mining fraternity.'

Wayne believes the government lost a once-in-a-lifetime opportunity. 'The government could also set up a treaty commission. It could set up a whole range of things. Why haven't they? Because they don't really give a shit about blackfellas. They don't care. And they want to acculturate us. Ultimately, it's all about assimilation and acculturation.'

Had the *Aboriginal Cultural Heritage Act 2021* been in place at the time of the diamond discovery around Barramundi Gap, or when Amax proposed to drill for oil on sacred land near Noonkanbah, or when Rio Tinto was considering the expansion of Brockman 4, it wouldn't have been sufficient to protect these sites. So, how far had Western Australia really come? How were Traditional Owners expected to move forward when the laws that governed them were still so entrenched in a racist past? For Wayne, the way forward lay in Aboriginal-led development. 'I just think the more we can build our own economic base, the better off we are. This government is asleep at the wheel.'

* * *

The racism which consistently undermined Indigenous aspirations was also highlighted for Wayne in 2020, when Traditional Owners put in a bid to buy Jubilee Downs cattle station, which incorporated the Quanbun Station lease. Quanbun was a storied place for Wayne—from falling in love, to falling out with his dad—it was the setting for many formative experiences. But for older Traditional Owners, the memories were much darker.

In *Noonkanbah*, Ginger Nganawilla told of how his father had got tired of working on Quanbun for rations and decided to take a break. The white boss put the police onto Ginger's dad. They caught up with him halfway to Cherrabun, tied him to a tree, took a lump of stone, and beat in his face and ribs and back until he couldn't walk (Hawke and Gallagher 51–52).

The Roth Report from 1905 also recorded atrocities practised by the white station owners: the women on Quanbun were whipped at night if they allowed the sheep to stray and were regularly stolen from their husbands and raped (*Royal Commission*).

So, when an opportunity arose to purchase Jubilee Downs and the Quanbun lease, Traditional Owners mustered forces to put in a bid. Yanunijarra Aboriginal Corporation, the Kimberley Agriculture and Pastoral Company (KAPCO) and The Nature Conservancy bid twenty-five million dollars for the property. They did this on behalf of all the Aboriginal families who had lived, worked and suffered on the country. They thought they were in with a good chance. KAPCO was performing well, running twenty-eight thousand cattle across four stations and boasting sixty-five percent Indigenous employment. The leases it held encompassed 130 kilometres of Martuwarra frontage; as an Aboriginal-owned company, it had defied the tyranny of low expectations and proved it was a force to be reckoned with.

Despite this, Traditional Owners were knocked out in the first round of bidding. The property was sold to Andrew 'Twiggy' Forrest, a billionaire with a long connection to the Kimberley. It was his great-great-uncle Alexander Forrest who was credited with first exploring the region and who went on to become involved in a meat ring of one hundred privileged people who held forty million acres of land in the Kimberley. Forrest told ABC Radio the purchase was 'deeply personal' and that his great-great-uncle had nearly lost his life in the region (Varischetti 03:17). He said it was his understanding the pastoralists hadn't used price as the only criterion for the sale. They wanted the new owners to be 'people who really love and care for the environment' (Varischetti 04:12–14).

It was a bitter blow for Traditional Owners.

Forrest spoke of the jobs he would create for local communities—throughout his career he had shown a firm commitment to supporting Indigenous education and training.

Wayne wanted to see a new era of Indigenous people taking control of the land and economic base.

'Traditional Owners no longer wish to work for white bosses. We've not received recognition, or compensation, for the loss of our traditional lands. We've been locked out of 139 years of economic opportunity. We've been made sit aside and watch pastoralists and other people use our land for economic benefit for their families, for the state and the nation. We've missed out on the opportunity to build intergenerational wealth. This purchase suggests the continuation of capital built off the back of Aboriginal land, at the expense of Aboriginal people. I'm disappointed that again, here was an opportunity for the state to intervene and hand back the property as part of a native title compensation and social justice package. Instead, it did nothing.'

* * *

The mercury soared, the air was sopping, and work slowed down. It was nearly the end of 2021. Traditional Owners faced an uncertain time ahead. The Kimberley was braced for sickness—not a wave of leprosy, or measles, but a wave of COVID-19. There was intense pressure on the Martuwarra (the Fitzroy River), the lifeblood of Nyikina country, not from the introduction of livestock, but from plans to tap the river for irrigation. There were concerns about climate change, about the effect of the new Aboriginal Cultural Heritage Act, about the indifference of the federal government to the Uluru Statement from the Heart, and about the region's chronic crime—a whole generation of Kimberley kids had dead eyes.

For over three decades, Wayne had been giving and giving and giving, and there was still so much to be done. In his old friend Clinton Wolf's view, Wayne was at the peak of his power, the best in his field. 'Wayne's quite unusual in that he can be a rainmaker. He knows how to come up with ideas and create positivity, and he can keep an eager eye on the backend and understand the intricacies of the business. In negotiations, others might say, *That deal's good enough, let's accept it.* But Wayne's ability to hold the line and hold his nerve is phenomenal. As far as I'm concerned, he's the best negotiator in Australia for getting the best deal for the mob. He is not the guy industry or government wants to see walking through the door representing the mob.'

But his eldest daughter, Sara, wondered if it wasn't perhaps time for her dad to think about himself for a moment, to think about his family, to think about retiring.

'He has spent his whole life fighting and hasn't received any kind of recognition for it. He's suffered from the tall poppy syndrome. I think retirement for Dad is going out and living on country, running a few cattle, growing bush foods, and setting up businesses that Jarred and Tessa can run. He wants to ensure our family has a strong connection to country. Dad loves being in the bush. When people say to him, *So, you studied law*, he's always quick to tell them he was a boilermaker first. He wants people to know he's a practical man.'

Wayne had come a long way from his childhood in Derby, a long way from contemplating suicide with his grandpa's gun. 'I wanted to escape the humiliation of being a ratbag kid. I'm so glad I didn't take the next step. I would have lost the opportunity to have these incredible experiences with my grandparents and parents, to be part of the Indigenous community and to make real change. Life is a journey—we have to acknowledge the downs, but we always need to be optimistic there's going to be an up.'

As a teenager, unable to read or write, Wayne never imagined the heights to which his career would soar. He would become a qualified lawyer and negotiate a 1.5 billion dollar compensation package for Traditional Owners, a feat that had never been done before and hasn't been repeated since. For a decade he would run a successful Aboriginal business. Ready for a new challenge, he would investigate ways to address the rampant youth crime in Broome and Derby, dreaming up a concept for a pastoral school on one of the KAPCO properties, which would enrol young people at risk of being sent to a juvenile detention facility in Perth. Chris says, 'If someone tells Wayne it can't be done, there's a problem that can't be fixed, he turns around and says, *Watch me*.'

With such a breadth of experience behind him, and a mind endlessly restless, the retirement option will likely be some years away yet. At fifty-two, Wayne's still on the boards of the Kimberley Land Council, Walalakoo Aboriginal Corporation and the Kimberley Agriculture and Pastoral Company. He's still running the *National Indigenous Times*. He aspires to own the first Aboriginal-controlled ASX-listed mining company. He's joined forces with some of the environmentalists who were his sworn enemies in the gas days—their values align on other issues. In his 'spare' time he tends bees. And he's just signed on as a Professor of Practice at UNSW's Business School. 'I feel like I've got so much in my head to teach people. There's no point it just sitting in my head. I want young people to consider whether I've got things right, or whether they could do this better.'

Perhaps Wayne's next logical step will be toward politics, though his wife, Chris, is not so sure. 'Maybe he's too wise to go into politics. He's able to make a bigger influence outside the system.

We've seen so many people crushed. And Wayne has had to choose work over family for so long. Maybe he'll do something where he doesn't get kicked all the time. Something for himself.' She's also fearful of his age—he's moving through his fifties. 'Wayne's uncles and grandfathers passed away in their fifties and sixties. We might not have much time left with him.'

Whichever direction his career takes from here, one thing that's certain is that his children share his vision. Sara says, 'Every time I feel shit about intergenerational trauma and Indigenous disadvantage, I remind myself that Aboriginal people have only been able to participate in society for just over fifty years—if we consider the 1967 referendum as a turning point in Indigenous rights. In just fifty years, in less than a generation, we've got Indigenous surgeons, psychologists, lawyers, CEOs and politicians in power. Indigenous people are very intellectual people and can make very difficult decisions when presented with all the right information. We make decisions based on the present, the past and the future. We look at the value proposition—what is the long-term benefit for my people? We ask—*how much do we need this?* Because development is often the only lever Indigenous people have to pull ourselves out of poverty and disadvantage and try and slingshot ourselves in some kind of way to participate in an economy that's actively excluded us for over a hundred years.'

Chris, too, has shared Wayne's vision and been his constant anchor—right back to that dusty and fateful bus ride to Adelaide, when the old women crooned love songs. Wayne says, 'Chris has been my absolute foundation. I could have never achieved half of what I've done without her. She has been my counsel, my adviser, my lover and best friend. And I'm not the most easy person to get on with, but she has come to the table with this gentle power, and she has pretty much influenced every aspect of my life, from the way I talk to my mob, to the way I present information, to the humbleness with which I have to deal with people who are not happy. She's made me wiser about the broader traumas that people carry.'

Wayne's old friend, mentor and chair from the KALACC days, Walmajarri man Joe Brown, says, 'Wayne's a family man now. He's got big kids himself. He's made a dad of himself and he's very strong.'

He pauses for a moment, reflecting on Wayne's remarkable journey.

Then he says, 'Yes, and he's still travelling.'

Notes

Prologue: Bilby killer

1 *The Native Title Act 1993* was passed by the federal parliament while Paul Keating was prime minister. It was one part of a three-part response to the landmark Mabo decision, which determined Australia was not terra nullius—a land belonging to no-one—at the time of European colonisation. The other two parts of this response were the creation of the Indigenous Land Fund and a social justice package—the latter was never implemented. Native title recognises that Aboriginal and Torres Strait Islander peoples have rights and interests to land and waters according to their traditional law and customs. These rights might include living on country and erecting shelters, visiting and protecting important sites for hunting, fishing, food gathering and medicine collection, or accessing country for traditional purposes, like ceremonies.

In 1998, the Coalition government led by Prime Minister John Howard pushed through a suite of amendments to the Act, commonly referred to as the '10 Point Plan'. These amendments watered down the original legislation. They included allowing the National Native Title Tribunal absolute authority over claims for native title, giving state governments power to extinguish native title over crown lands for matters of 'national interest', and removing the right to claim native title in or around urban areas. Indigenous land use agreements were created to promote coexistence. The amendments made the process for groups to claim native title more difficult.

To gain native title, Aboriginal people need to prove they have had a continuous and unbroken connection to their country since colonisation. In the Kimberley this can be problematic, considering the children taken from their mothers and sent to the missions, the movement of people off country and onto pastoral stations, and the forced removal of people from pastoral stations into towns. For Wayne's group, Nyikina Mangala, the process to gain native title recognition took eighteen years. Many of the old people who initiated the claim are no longer with us.

Once native title is determined, a prescribed body corporate (PBC) is established. Those Traditional Owners on the board of the PBC are often the first point of contact for outside interests wishing to access land. They help manage and protect native title interests for their broader native title group.

It's important to understand, particularly within the context of Wayne's story, that native title does not give Traditional Owners the power of veto when it comes to development. What are available to Traditional Owners are procedural rights, which can cause significant project delays and can help put pressure on companies to better compensate Traditional Owners over terms of access. Generally, if there's a proposal to deal with land that will affect native title rights and interests—like compulsory acquisition or the grant of a mining tenement—then this is called a future act. There are times when the government and outside party (like a proponent) may be required to negotiate for at least six months with Traditional Owners, with a view to reaching agreement about terms of access. There are other instances when it's decided that native title rights and interests won't be affected, and these attract the 'expedited procedure' process.

In 142 future act determinations, the National Native Title Tribunal has only found in favour of Traditional Owners three times. That means that only three times has it been determined that 'the act may not be done'.

More information on Indigenous land use agreements and future acts is available on the National Native Title Tribunal's website, nntt.gov.au.

1: With rosaries in one hand, revolvers in the other

2   In various historical records Guirella's name is spelled differently. I've kept the spelling from Cornish's diary here.

3   According to Albert Archer's son, the late Cyril Archer, Albert too had an Indian father. It's possible Wayne's great-grandmother Jira and Albert Archer were half siblings.

4   Ian Crawford writes in *We Won the Victory* that the Walambi people were to the south and the Kulari (a collective term for the Ganbera and Wunambal) were to the west.

5   For the full and nuanced story of the Mowla Bluff massacre, please refer to John Darraga Watson's *Never Stand Still: Stories of Life, Land and Politics in the Kimberley*, his chapter in *Raparapa: Stories from the Fitzroy River Drovers*, and *Whispering in Our Hearts*, a film directed by Mitch Torres and produced by Graeme Isaac.

6   'Gin' was once a term used by whitefellas to describe Aboriginal women. It's highly offensive.

2: The shadows that don't exist

7   Mangkaja Arts began as an arm of Karrayili Adult Education Centre. It became incorporated as a separate organisation in 1993. 'Mangkaja' was named by Kumanjayi (deceased) Skipper. It comes from a Walmajarri word for the shelters erected in the Great Sandy Desert during the wet season. See mangkaja.com/about.

3: If you can make it in Fitzroy, you can make it anywhere

8   The Aboriginal and Torres Strait Islander Commission (ATSIC) was established by Bob Hawke's Labor government. It ran from 1990 to 2005 and was the organisation through which Aboriginal and Torres Strait Islander people were formally involved in government processes that had bearing on their lives.

4: The front line and the battleline

9   Queenie McKenzie offers a slightly different version of this story in *From Digging Sticks to Writing Sticks: Stories of Kija Women*. (Thomas et al.), p.136.

5: Every strong life calls forth enemies

10 Initially there were fifteen groups; later, Djabera Djabera became absorbed by Jabirr Jabirr / Goolarabooloo.

11 Usually, KLC's AGMs were conducted on country and spanned several days, incorporating the annual general meetings of the Kimberley Aboriginal Law and Culture Centre and the Kimberley Language Resource Centre.

6: I challenge anyone to take that kind of fire

12 The Boulevard is one of the main shopping centres in Broome, air-conditioned, with a Woolworths and several big retailers.

13 Lily O'Neill writes that the agreements were subsequently signed in June 2011. While they were supposed to be Indigenous Land Use Agreements, the split in claim group meant authorisation and registration procedures were too hard to satisfy. So the agreements were made as a 'future act' agreement under s.31 of the *Native Title Act 1993* instead.

7: Work hard, have fun, get shit done

14 KRED originally stood for Kimberley Regional Economic Development. Later this was dropped and the company was referred to simply as 'KRED Enterprises'.

15 Hayley doesn't recall Wayne introducing her as a 'junkyard dog'! She says it was something like 'Nyikina Mangala's secret weapon'. Either way, she remembers John Watson seemed amused.

Works cited

Australian Human Rights Commission. 'Native Title Report 2006: Chapter 5: The Argyle Participation Agreement.' humanrights. gov.au/our-work/native-title-report-2006-chapter-5-argyle-participation-agreement.

Baker, Richard. Episode One, 'Wrong Skin.' *Sydney Morning Herald*, 14 Jul. 2018, theage.com.au/national/episode-one-richard-and-julie-20180711-p4zque.html.

—, Richard. Episode Five, 'Winners and Losers.' *Sydney Morning Herald*, 27 Jul. 2018, smh.com.au/national/episode-five-winners-and-losers-20180712-p4zr2g.html.

—, Richard. 'Native Entitlement: Wheeling and Dealing in the Kimberley.' *Sydney Morning Herald*, 27 Jul. 2018, smh.com.au/wrong-skin/native-entitlement-wheeling-and-dealing-in-the-kimberley-20180724-p4ztd2.html.

'Barnett Blames Indigenous Community for Failed Gas Deal.' *ABC News*, 20 Sep. 2008, abc.net.au/news/2008-09-20/barnett-blames-indigenous-community-for-failed-gas/516202.

Benedictine Community of New Norcia. 'Drysdale River Mission.' *St Ildephonsus College Magazine*, New Norcia, WA, Benedictine Community, 1930.

Bergmann, Wayne. 'Opinion: Aboriginal Heritage Bill Continues in the West Australian Parliament.' *National Indigenous Times*,

22 Nov. 2021, nit.com.au/opinion-aboriginal-heritage-bill-continues-in-the-western-australian-parliament.

Botsman, Peter. 'Law Below the Top Soil.' *Walmadany (James Price Point) and the Question of the Browse Basin Gas Resources of North West Australia*. Save The Kimberley, 2012.

Bradshaw, Elizabeth, and Rachel Fry. 'A Management Report for the Lurujarri Heritage Trail, Broome.' Western Australia Department of Aboriginal Sites, Western Australian Museum, Perth, 1989.

'Browse [Land] Agreement Bill 2012.' Extract from *Hansard*, Western Australian Parliament, 30 Nov. 2012, parliament.wa.gov.au/Hansard%5Chansard.nsf/0/d4f360ce9e85e1d748257afc0028eb0c.

Bullimore, Kim. 'Media Dreaming: Representation of Aboriginality in Modern Australian Media.' *Asia Pacific Media Educator*, vol. 6, 1999, ro.uow.edu.au/cgi/viewcontent.cgi?article=1265&context=apme.

Cornish, Hamlet. *Pioneering in the Kimberleys*. Hesperian Press, 2011.

Cousins, Geoff. 'Woodside Would Do Well to Dump Gas Hub Hubris.' *Weekend Australian*, 24–25 Sep. 2011.

Crawford, Ian. *We Won the Victory*. Fremantle Arts Centre Press, 2001.

Daisy Lungunan & Ors on Behalf of the Nyikina & Mangala Native Title Claimants/Western Australia/William Robert Richmond. [2013] NNTTA 112, www8.austlii.edu.au/cgi-bin/viewdoc/au/cases/cth/NNTTA/2013/112.html.

Dick, T. 'Hard Bargaining.' *Broome Advertiser*, 12 Sep. 2002.

Dumont, Eugenie. *Heritage Fight*. 24 May 2016, *Vimeo*, vimeo.com/ondemand/heritagefight2.

'Eminent Australians Pen Open Letter to the WA Premier on Aboriginal Cultural Heritage Bill.' *National Indigenous Times*, 30 Nov. 2021, nit.com.au/exclusive-eminent-australians-pen-open-letter-to-the-wa-premier-on-aboriginal-cultural-heritage-bill.

'Fallout Continues Over Inpex Decision to Move to NT.' *ABC News*, 27 Sep. 2008, abc.net.au/news/2008-09-27/fallout-continues-over-inpex-decision-to-move-to-nt/523614.

Flint, David. 'Is it Time to Sue over Mabo?' *The Australian*, 10 Feb. 2006.

Forrest, Alexander. *North-West Exploration: Journal of Expedition from DeGrey River to Port Darwin*. Richard Pether, 1880.

—, Alexander. Western Australian Parliamentary Debates, 4 Oct. 1893, no. 5, p. 1052. parliament.wa.gov.au/Hansard/hansard1870to1995.nsf/83cc4ce93b5d4e0b48257b33001cfef6/F8AD89122BA5B88648257A4F00121C22/$File/18931004_Assembly.pdf.

'Forrest Backs Barnett's Dubai Plan.' *The Sydney Morning Herald*, 22 Sep. 2008, smh.com.au/national/forrest-backs-barnetts-dubai-plan-20080922-4lg4.html.

Fox, Joe. *The Shield and the Spear*. Magabala Books, 2022.

Godbehear, Harold S. *Kimberley Was God's*. Hesperian Press, 2011.

Hawke, Steve, and Michael Gallagher. *Noonkanbah*. Fremantle Arts Centre Press, 1989.

'Heritage Trail Lurujarri. Retracing the Song Cycle from Minarriny to Yinara.' Heritage Council of Western Australia, 1999, goolarabooloo.org.au/downloads/Lurujarri_Trail_broshure.pdf.

Hingston, C. 'Council votes on LNG.' *Broome Advertiser*. 13 Nov. 2008, p. 1.

Hingston, Chris, and Ben Jones. 'Former Judge Taken to Task.' *Broome Advertiser*, 18 Feb. 2010, p. 1.

'"I'm No Coconut!" Gas Hub Dispute Turns Ugly as Angry Carol Martin Declares "I'll Sue for Racist Slander".' *National Indigenous Times*. 28 Sep. 2011.

'Indigenous Business Growth: Working Together to Realise Potential.' Supply Nation. First Australians Capital. 2018, supplynation.org.au/wp-content/uploads/2018/10/Building-Indigenous-Growth-Report.pdf.

'Inquiry into the Destruction of 46,000 Year Old Caves at the Juukan Gorge in the Pilbara Region of Western Australia.' Law Council of Australia, 21 Aug. 2020, lawcouncil.asn.au/publicassets/24891840-2ef3-ea11-9434-005056be13b5/3864.

Isdell, James. 'Travelling Protectors' Reports', *Report of the Chief Protector of Aborigines for the Year Ending 30th June, 1908*. Perth, 1909.

—, James. 'Travelling Protectors' Reports', *Report of the Chief Protector of Aborigines for the Year Ending 30th June, 1909*. Perth, 1909.

Karp, Paul. 'Scott Morrison Claims Indigenous Voice to Parliament Would be a Third Chamber.' *The Guardian*, 26 Sep. 2018, theguardian.com/australia-news/2018/sep/26/scott-morrison-claims-indigenous-voice-to-parliament-would-be-a-third-chamber.

Kimberley Land Council newsletter, 1978.

'KLC Calls for Aboriginal Heritage Act Rewrite.' Kimberley Land Council, 29 May 2021, klc.org.au/klc-calls-for-aboriginal-heritage-act-rewrite.

Klinger, Peter. 'Putting Fizz into Woodside Wasn't Easy: Voelte.' *The West Australian*, 3 Jun. 2011, thewest.com.au/news/wa/putting-fizz-into-woodside-wasnt-easy-voelte-ng-ya-166379.

La Fontaine, Monique. *New Legend: A Story of Law and Culture and the Fight for Self-Determination in the Kimberley*. Kimberley Aboriginal Law and Culture Centre, 2006.

Laurie, Victoria. 'Kimberley Braces for Call of Progress.' *The Australian*, 27 Dec. 2008.

'LNG Precinct Legislation Introduced to Parliament.' Government of Western Australia, 20 Sep. 2012, mediastatements.wa.gov.au/Pages/Barnett/2012/09/LNG-Precinct-legislation-introduced-to-Parliament.aspx.

Manning, Paddy. 'WA to Change the Face of the Kimberley Forever.' *Sydney Morning Herald*, 5 Sep. 2009, smh.com.au/business/wa-to-change-the-face-of-the-kimberley-forever-20090904-fbev.html.

Marchant, Leslie R. *Aboriginal Administration in Western Australia, 1886–1905*. Australian Institute of Aboriginal Studies, 1981.

McGeough, Paul. 'At Breaking Point.' *The Weekend West*, 20 Nov. 2010.

McGinty, Sue, et al. *Karrayili: Adult Education in a Remote Australian Community*. Aboriginal Studies Press, 2000.

Medhora, Shalailah. 'Remote Communities are "Lifestyle Choices" says Tony Abbott.' *The Guardian*, 10 Mar. 2015, theguardian.com/australia-news/2015/mar/10/remote-communities-are-lifestyle-choices-says-tony-abbott.

Milgin, Annie, and Liz Thompson. 'The Story of Woonyoomboo.' *ABC Radio National*, 6 Jun. 2017.

'Minnie-Pool Charley, a Few Remarks About the Customs, &c., of the Natives of West Kimberley.' *Eastern Districts Chronicle*, 18 Nov. 1893.

'Missy Higgins Clip'. *YouTube*, uploaded by *Wilderness Society*, 22 Dec. 2008, youtube.com/watch?v=l2V5G4r9p8I&feature=emb_logo (private link).

Mjöberg, Eric. *Among Wild Animals and People in Australia. Bland Vilda Djur och Folk i Australien*. Hesperian Press, 2012.

Native Affairs Personal File. Department of Native Affairs *H/C Fulgentius or Fred Fraser of Derby – Personal File*, Cons 1351, 1940/0945.

'Never Again: Inquiry into the destruction of 46,000 year old caves at the Juukan Gorge in the Pilbara region of Western Australia – Interim

Report.' Parliament of the Commonwealth of Australia, 2020, apo. org.au/sites/default/files/resource-files/2020-12/apo-nid310049.pdf.

'Northern Development Taskforce to Guide Kimberley Development.' Government of Western Australia, 11 Jul. 2007, mediastatements.wa.gov.au/Pages/Carpenter/2007/07/Northern-Development-Taskforce-to-guide-Kimberley-development.aspx.

'Northern Development Taskforce – Browse Basin Gas.' Extract from *Hansard*, Western Australian Government.
20 Nov. 2007, parliament.wa.gov.au/Hansard/hansard.nsf/0/b7716d1888761604c8257570007f828b.

Northern Development Taskforce: Site Evaluation Report, Part A. Western Australian Government Department of Industry and Resources, 2008.

Northern Development Taskforce: Site Evaluation Report, Part B. Western Australian Government Department of Industry and Resources, 2008.

O'Neill, Lily. 'The Bindunbur "Bombshell": The True Traditional Owners of James Price Point and the Politics of the Anti-Gas Protest.' *University of New South Wales Law Journal*, vol. 42, no. 2, 2019, pp. 597–618, doi.org/10.53637/XBVY3708.

Owen, Chris. *Every Mother's Son is Guilty: A History of Policing in the Kimberley*. UWA Publishing, 2016, pp. 280–281.

Parker, Gareth, and Amy Williams. 'Police Brush Past Gas Protesters.' *The West Australian*, 5 Jul. 2011, thewest.com.au/news/australia/police-brush-past-gas-protesters-ng-ya-161849.

Parliamentary Debates Hansard, Thirty-Ninth Parliament First Session, Western Australian Parliament, 23 Oct. 2013, parliament.wa.gov.au/Hansard/Hansard.nsf/0/ba810f5222876fd048257c0f00219876.

Peatling, Stephanie. 'Fear of Native Title Land Grab in Cities.' *Sydney Morning Herald*, 22 Sep. 2006.

Perez, Eugene. *Kalumburu, Formerly Drysdale River, Benedictine Mission North-Western Australia: A Golden Jubilee Publication (1908–1958)*. Abbey Press, 1958.

Prior, Flip. 'Aboriginal Protesters Are Not Bludgers.' *Broome Advertiser*, 16 Oct. 2011, thewest.com.au/news/kimberley/aboriginal-protesters-are-not-bludgers-ng-ya-147016.

—, Flip. 'In Derby, They Fear Weekends, and Who's Next.' *The West Australian*, 4 Aug. 2011. thewest.com.au/news/australia/in-derby-they-fear-weekends-and-whos-next-ng-ya-157656.

—, Flip. 'Outrage Over Gas Move.' *Broome Advertiser*, 9 Sep. 2010.

Puertollano, Aggie. Private recording. Interview conducted by Wayne's sister Helen. 1995.

'Review of the *Aboriginal Heritage Act 1972 (WA)*.' Kimberley Land Council, 2018, wa.gov.au/system/files/2021-05/Submission-058-Kimberley-Land-Council.pdf.

RMIT ABC Fact Check. 'Pauline Hanson Says a Lot of People Been Dispossessed of Their Lands Due to the Mabo Decision. Is She Correct?' *ABC News*, 29 Aug. 2019, abc.net.au/news/2019-08-29/fact-check-mabo-decision-high-court-dispossession-pauline-hanson/11342504.

Roe v State of Western Australia (No 2). [2011] FCA 102, pp. 122–24, jade.io/article/209912.

Roth Report, The. **See** *Royal Commission on the Condition of the Natives*.

Royal Commission on the Condition of the Natives, 1905. Perth, 1905, (The Roth Report), nla.gov.au/nla.obj-61348422/view?partId=nla.obj-61387674#.

Sampi, Patrick. 'Hope With No Return. The Story About My Son.' *Boab Battler*, 21 Apr. 1988.

'Shoulder to Shoulder.' Nyikina Mangala Pastoral Aboriginal Corporation Development Plan for Myroodah Station, May 2002.

Skyring, Fiona. 'Draft 7. Argyle Diamond Mine: Supplementary History Report. The Glen Hill Agreement 1980.' Oct. 2002. Prepared for Kimberley Land Council.

Spencer, Ben. 'Broome Ready for Fight as Gas Hub Polarises Town.' *The West Australian*, 3 Jan. 2009, pp.12–13.

Stratton, Rodney. *KRED*. 28 Nov. 2011, *Vimeo*, vimeopro.com/rodneystratton/rodney-stratton-1/video/32767189.

'Submission in Response to the Northern Development Taskforce Report.' Kimberley Land Council, 11 Nov. 2008.

Sullivan, Patrick. 'Policy Change and the Indigenous Land Corporation.' *AIATSIS Research Discussion Paper*, no. 25, AIATSIS, 2009.

'The Elders' Report into Preventing Indigenous Self-harm & Youth Suicide.' *Culture is Life*, Analysis & Policy Observatory (APO), 2014, apo.org.au/node/40060.

'The West Australian Nigger.' *Western Mail* [Perth], 14 Aug. 1886.

Thomas, Wil. 'LNG Debate. Opinion.' *Broome Advertiser,* 29 Jan. 2009.

Torres, Fulgentius. *The Torres Diaries 1901–1914: Diaries from Dom Fulgentius (Anthony) Torres Y Mayans, O.S.B., Abbot Nullius of New Norcia Bishop Titular of Dorylaeum Administrator Apostolic of the Kimberley Vicariate in North Western Australia.* Translated by Dom Eugene Perez, Artlook Books, 1987.

Varischetti, Belinda. 'Western Australia Country Hour.' *ABC News*, 9 Jul. 2020, abc.net.au/radio/programs/wa-country-hour/wa-country-hour/12418738.

Vaughan, Robert. 'Opinion.' *Broome Advertiser*, 23 Oct. 2008.

Wahlquist, Calla. 'Turnbull's Uluru Statement Rejection is "Mean-spirited Bastardry" – legal expert.' *The Guardian*, 26 Oct. 2017, theguardian.com/australia-news/2017/oct/26/turnbulls-uluru-statement-rejection-mean-spirited-bastardry-legal-expert.

Watson, John Darraga. *Never Stand Still: Stories of Life, Land and Politics in the Kimberley.* Jarlmadangah Burru Aboriginal Corporation, 2012.

Watson, John, et al. *Raparapa: Stories from the Fitzroy River Drovers.* Magabala Books, 2011.

Wicks v The Queen (1989). 44 A Crim R 147, WA Court of Criminal Appeal.

Wilcox, Murray. *Kimberley at the Crossroads: The Case Against the Gas Plant.* Save The Kimberley Ltd, 2010.

Wynne, Emma. 'Bringing the Wadjuk Spirits to Rest on Rottnest Island.' *ABC Radio Perth*, 9 Jan. 2015. abc.net.au/news/2015-01-09/bringing-the-wadjuk-spirits-to-rest-on-rottnest-island/6008936.

Yungngora Community of Noonkanbah Station, translation of the Walmajarri text of a petition to the Parliament of Western Australia, trans. Olive Bieundurry. Tabled in Hansard by Ron Davies, Leader of the Opposition, 17 May 1979: 1554–1555. parliament.wa.gov.au/Hansard/hansard1870to1995.nsf/83cc4ce93b5d4e0b48257b33001cfef6/E40293D50C60997048257A4500322F38/$File/19790517_Assembly.pdf.

Select bibliography

Balagai, Remi, et al. *This Is Your Place: Beagle Bay Mission, 1890–1990: Birthplace and Cradle of Catholic Presence in the Kimberley*. Beagle Bay Community, 1990.

Benterrak, Krim, et al. *Reading the Country*. Fremantle Arts Centre Press, 1996.

Choo, Christine. *Mission Girls: Aboriginal Women on Catholic Missions in the Kimberley, Western Australia, 1900–1950*. University of Western Australia Press, 2001.

Doohan, Kim. *Making Things Come Good: Relations between Aborigines and Miners at Argyle*. Backroom Press, 2008.

'Exile and the Kingdom – Part 1.' *Pakam*. 1992, ictv.com.au/video/item/1063.

'Exile and the Kingdom – Part 2.' *Pakam*. 1992, ictv.com.au/video/item/1064.

Green, Neville. *The Forrest River Massacres*. Fremantle Arts Centre Press, 1995.

—, Neville. *The Oombulgurri Story*. Focus Education Services, 1988.

Hawke, Steve. *A Town is Born: The Fitzroy Crossing Story*. Magabala Books, 2013.

Kelly, Damian. *James Price Point: The Story of a Movement. A Photographic Essay by Damian Kelly with Writings from the Campaign*. Damian Kelly Photography, 2016.

Kennedy, Peter. *Tales from Boomtown: Western Australian Premiers from Brand to Barnett*. UWA Publishing, 2014.

Mahood, Kim. *Position Doubtful*. Scribe Publications, 2016.

—, Kim. *Craft for a Dry Lake*. Penguin, 2000.

McGlade, Hannah, and Jeannine Purdy. '"No Jury Will Convict": An Account of Racial Killings in Western Australia.' *Studies in Western Australian History*, no. 22, 2001, DOI: 10.3316/ielapa.200113323, pp. 91–106.

O'Neill, Lily. *A Tale of Two Agreements: Negotiating Aboriginal Land Access Agreements in Australia's Natural Gas Industry*. The University of Melbourne, 2016, PhD Thesis.

Owen, Chris. "The Police Appear to be a Useless Lot up There": Law and Order in the East Kimberley 1884–1905.' *Aboriginal History Journal*, vol. 27, 2003.

Pike, Jimmy, and Pat Lowe. *You Call It Desert—We Used to Live There*. Magabala Books, Broome, 2010.

Roe, Paddy. *Gularabulu: Stories from the West Kimberley*. UWA Publishing, 2016.

Solonec, Cindy. *Debesa: The Story of Frank and Katie Rodriguez*. Magabala Books, 2021.

Solonec, Jacinta. *Shared Lives on Nigena Country: A Joint Biography of Katie and Frank Rodriguez, 1944–1994*. Edith Cowan University, 1994, api.research-repository.uwa.edu.au/ws/portalfiles/portal/9760025/Solonec_Jacinta_2015.pdf, PhD Thesis.

'The Crocodile Hole Report.' Kimberley Land Council and Waringarri Resource Centre, 1991.

Thomas, Mary, Veronica Ryan, Eileen Bray and Catholic Education Office (Perth, WA). *From Digging Sticks to Writing Sticks: Stories of Kija Women as told to Veronica Ryan/Translations by Eileen Bray and*

Mary Thomas. Catholic Education Office of Western Australia, 2001.

Woorunmurra, Banjo, and Howard Pedersen. *Jandamarra and the Bunuba Resistance*. Magabala Books, 2011.

Zucker, Margaret. 'Open Hearts: The Catholic Church and the Stolen Generation in the Kimberley.' *Journal of the Australian Catholic Historical Society*, vol. 29, 2008, pp. 23–37.

Acknowledgements

This project was made possible by the Australian Government's Regional Arts Fund, which supports the arts in regional and remote Australia, and by a grant from the Neilma Sidney Literary Travel Fund.

In my work life I owe a great debt to the incredible people who have been part of my team—who have given their all and then more by going above and beyond what is required to make a difference. I am forever grateful and thankful to Madelaine Dickie for believing in this story and giving time and energy to make this a reality.

There are many close friends who were there to support me when I needed help and guidance that gave me the strength to get up each day and keep pushing: Clinton Wolf, Ciaran O'Faircheallaigh, Jodie Pincini, Zoe Ramsay, Hayley Haas, Anthony Watson, Robert Watson, Patrick Green, Jennifer Allen and Phil Docherty are just a few to name.

—Wayne Bergmann

Acknowledgements

I'd like to thank everyone who contributed to Wayne's story in either a formal or informal way. There are those whose voices you've heard in the preceding pages. Their memories and wisdom ring strong—thank you all for giving us permission to use your quotes. There have also been many people behind the scenes who you haven't heard from but who made a valuable contribution to this book by way of historical materials, knowledge, photographs and memories. They include the late Derby elder Cyril Archer, Mary Anne Jebb, Joe Fox, Chris Owen, Malcolm Lindsay, Wil Thomas, Jill Pagnoccolo, Joyce Hudson, Damian Kelly, Jemma Arman, Thomas Saunders, Paul Gamblin, Tom Vigilante and Carolyn Pickett. I'd like to thank the whole team at Exmouth Library for sourcing rare texts for me and for creating a space in which I always felt welcome to work. Wayne's story also benefited from an Australian Society of Authors mentorship. I had the fortune to be paired up with John Zubrzycki—a brilliant author, researcher and former foreign correspondent—who guided the development of early drafts with fresh and thoughtful insights. Thank you to Mum, Dad, my sister, Charlotte, and my husband, Tom, for your deep understanding of the importance of this story. Finally, it's such pleasure to be working with Fremantle Press again. Wayne's book is in steady hands with Georgia Richter, Anne Ryden, Claire Miller and Chloe Walton, as it makes its exhilarating journey from editing, through to publication and beyond!

—Madelaine Dickie

Also available from fremantlepress.com.au

Five years after first living in the Indian Ocean Territories, Reneé Pettitt-Schipp finds herself returning, haunted by memories of the asylum seekers she taught there in Australia's detention system. Why do the islands still have a hold on her? Why are her memories such troubled ones? And why can she not let go?

Closer to Indonesia than Australia, Christmas Island and Cocos (Keeling) Islands are out of sight and out of mind to most Australians, but they are the sites of some of our frontier wars, the places where our identity is laid bare in all its flawed complexity—and the places where there is time and space enough to ask: can we be better than this?

… *a travel narrative, a memoir, and an impressively researched history of a place too often overlooked.* Weekend Australian

This book is carefully crafted, thought-provoking and enlightening… a must-read for general readers and anyone interested in Australian national identity, politics, humanitarian issues and social justice. Five Stars! Australian Rural & Regional News

and all good bookstores

www.ingramcontent.com/pod-product-compliance
Lightning Source LLC
Chambersburg PA
CBHW031426150426
43191CB00006B/415